WHY
V**O**TE
2015
GREEN

EDITED BY
SHAHRAR ALI

WITH A FOREWORD BY
JENNY JONES

\B^b\
Biteback Publishing

First published in Great Britain in 2015 by
Biteback Publishing Ltd
Westminster Tower
3 Albert Embankment
London SE1 7SP

ISBN 978-1-84954-840-3
10 9 8 7 6 5 4 3 2 1

A CIP catalogue record for this book is available from the British Library.

Set in Chaparral Pro

Printed and bound in Great Britain by
CPI Group (UK) Ltd, Croydon CR0 4YY

Life is rich

For

Sevara, my soul

Shalir, our son

Contents

Foreword – Jenny Jones   vii

Chapter 1   Green Values – Shahrar Ali   1

Chapter 2   Climate Change – David Flint   17

Chapter 3   Economy – Molly Scott Cato   32

Chapter 4   Education – Martin Francis   42

Chapter 5   Women's Politics – Sarah Cope   56

Chapter 6   Welfare – Noel Lynch   69

Chapter 7   Home Affairs – Peter Cranie   79

Chapter 8   Young People and Politics – Amelia Womack   87

Chapter 9   Constitutional Reform – Adam Ramsay   97

Chapter 10   Housing – Tom Chance   108

Chapter 11   Transport – Caroline Russell   121

Chapter 12   Environment – Shasha Khan   130

Chapter 13   International Affairs – Tony Clarke   140

Chapter 14   Animals – Caroline Allen   152

Appendix   The Green Party's Core Values   165

Acknowledgements   167

About the Editor   168

Foreword

JENNY JONES

The next parliament is crucial for a secure future. We face three crises, each of which will come to a head in the next five years.

First, our planet is threatened by rapidly increasing climate change. Unless we can reverse the growth of emissions within the next parliament and reach international agreement, it will become ever harder, and perhaps impossible, to keep the problem within manageable bounds.

Secondly, the financial crash and austerity policies have worsened inequality, increased poverty and driven many people to the edge of despair. Unless these policies are reversed, and soon, there will be great destruction to our social fabric. Many people will suffer poverty and even starvation, and there's a real threat of major unrest.

Thirdly, our political institutions are shown to be increasingly inadequate. The first-past-the-post system is wholly inappropriate to a politics of five or more parties. The House of Lords is a privileged anachronism. Many Scots are dissatisfied with the Union. Besides this, overall democracy is threatened by the increasing power of corporate interests, operating both as political lobbyists and in negotiating treaties that will give them a veto power over national and EU institutions.

All of these things may have gone past the point of no return by 2020. But there is an alternative. Increasing numbers of people are mobilising against climate change. Increasing numbers of people reject the austerity agenda. Increasing numbers of people see the inadequacies in our political system. These people often think that all the parties are the same and that there is no one to vote for.

Fortunately, they are wrong. The Green Party sees the crises clearly and has the policies to address all three of them. Greens would prioritise effective action against climate change; we would reverse the austerity policies of all the grey parties; we would make fundamental reforms to our political and constitutional system. We would help ensure a viable future for generations to come.

If you want to play a part in solving these problems, you must vote Green.

Baroness Jenny Jones AM
January 2015

Chapter 1

Green Values

SHAHRAR ALI

Core values

It has become a truism that to serve the people well a political party must offer change. But we must ask who benefits from this change and how its success can be measured. Success could be measured as the winning of an election, no matter who else loses. In this case, the offer of change is simply a means to winning and therefore a candidate would be willing to say or do anything – falsely promising change – just to get elected. Thus the currency of politics gets devalued. Politics becomes a game that serves only its key players. From the fiddling of expense claims and misappropriation of second-home allowances to the award of a peerage to a favoured party donor, politics is diminished through self-interest and mutual back-scratching.

Green politics is anything but a game. It's a noble pursuit, not a dark art. It's a vocation, not a career. It's about treating people as worthy in themselves, not as a means to an end. It's about caring and acting for future people, non-human animals and other species. The change on offer is to obtain the collective good of the people, by consent. The decisions and actions of politicians are hugely consequential – for people and planet. While competitive instincts can come into play, one could not do justice to the task of governing a country by regarding the ends as the winning of power for the sake of it. On the contrary, in politics today it is precisely those 'ends' that are now up for grabs.

This volume introduces 'the collection of goods to which Green politics aims', in the words of Greens. If you are a prospective voter then I hope you will find this an invaluable resource that brings together key Green Party policies, and articulates reasons for them, without some of the limitations of an official election manifesto. I have asked contributors not to refrain from using their own voice and I'm proud to share with you what they have produced. I want us to be heard, in all our diversity. There is a consistency of approach and value to be found across green manifestos, which I hope enables you to anticipate where you stand with us, and us with you – a relationship of trust. This volume attempts to start building that relationship by articulating what we stand for.

In this introduction, I refer to the Core Values of the Philosophical Basis of the Green Party of England and Wales. Our sister parties in Scotland and Northern Ireland enjoy autonomy, but their approach is the same, as is the consensus evidenced by green parties internationally. The Core Values consists of ten paragraphs, drafted and agreed by our members and open to revision at future conferences. I've included it at the end of the book and you are invited to refer to it at any time.

Ours is an inspiring declaration of dissent from the status quo, commitment to noble goals and ambition for a revitalised political order. The use of demonstratives – 'should', 'must', 'cannot' – is telling. Ours is not an exercise in short-term political expediency, or a desire to avoid judgements for fear of being labelled do-gooders. Ours is a conviction that politics is, and should be, about universal truths: our dependence on planetary life-support systems; recognition of the consequences of our failure to manage resources sustainably; and obligations to our contemporaries, future generations and other animals.

I've met many a party member who joined as a result of reading the Core Values. They've identified with the party through ideals rather than through possession of a card (which we don't issue as such). The false offer of change devalues politics precisely because in politics right values are so important. Meaningful change requires allegiance to the right values.

Philosophical basis

I'm an advocate of critical thinking. Politicians who make decisions on the basis of bad inference are more likely to get things wrong. Colin Powell, at the UN in 2003, begged the question when he argued for military intervention: 'War is a last resort; but it must be a resort.' Nobody was disputing that a last resort was also a resort, but the question was whether that point had been reached. Powell assumed the thing he was meant to prove. Perhaps he was determined to pursue war regardless, but it would have been useful for those present to have exposed his faulty reasoning.

Having a philosophical basis demonstrates our desire for ethical rigour. No other party speaks of such a thing; yet the idea that politics should be grounded in ethics is not novel. The clue is in the title: Conservative Party has come to mean small government and less tax; Labour Party – protecting workers' rights; Liberal Democrats – liberty and democracy; UKIP – separation from the political union of the EU. Politicians have not always stuck to the idea embedded within their party name. Under Blair, Labour betrayed its welfarist roots, adopting free market reforms to the detriment of public services and the disbenefit of the poor. That Labour can now quite credibly be labelled Conservative devalues them politically and undermines any claim for them to be able to speak as they find things.

Green politics isn't only about greening the environment, reducing our negative impact on the biosphere or sustaining our resources. Though it certainly is these things, it's also about much more. What

ultimate values underpin green philosophy as contained in the statement of Core Values? How may we illuminate their content? There
are three: inclusivity, equality and right means.

Inclusivity

Green politics isn't just about you and me, or even just about human
beings at large; it's also about future generations and other species.
Let's look at three claims contained in the Core Values:

ANTI-DISCRIMINATION

*'A healthy society is … free from discrimination whether based on race,
colour, gender, sexual orientation, religion, social origin or any other
prejudice.'*

The Green Party is opposed to all forms of discrimination. The list
of characteristics to which prejudice may be encountered in society
is not intended to be exhaustive. Gender should not be interpreted,
say, as only of the man/woman binary sort, but includes all. The
LGBTIQ group in our party – lesbian, gay, bisexual, trans, intersex
and queer – lends a focus to tackling discrimination. We work to
ensure that everybody in society is valued, respected and empowered, regardless of their sexuality or gender identity. With regard to
religious belief, we accept that lack of belief is also not a ground for
discrimination. We emphasise all-inclusivity in society and intolerance of prejudice of all sorts.

MATERIAL SECURITY AND FUTURE GENERATIONS

*'Every person, in this and future generations, should be entitled to basic
material security as of right.'*

This statement relates to the rights of our contemporaries and future
generations. Both groups can make a legitimate demand of us, which

we are hardly satisfying as a society. Today, poverty exists in the UK and abroad: the first is relative, the second absolute, but both are real. In the UK, we can define poverty qualitatively as the deprivation and exclusion from certain goods that have become customary in society, including basic needs and fair access to them. Quantitatively, a low income threshold for a family will make it predictable that they lack the resources available for achieving a basic standard of living. The number of UK households below average income has increased, judged against a baseline that remains fixed over the time under review. Unfortunately, this government tries to massage the figures by using a baseline that shifts, such that when average income goes down, some of those in relative poverty can perversely be declared as above the line even though their living circumstances have not changed. In 2014, UNICEF published the report 'Children of the Recession: The impact of the economic crisis on child well-being in rich countries', which listed the UK twenty-fifth on a league table of forty-one countries. Those in relative poverty in the UK increased from 24.0 to 25.6 per cent over the period 2008–12. This is the reality of child poverty in the UK. More than one in four children experiences it. At the sharp end, many of our children are going hungry or cold in today's austerity Britain. Relative poverty has become severe in its own right.

Absolute poverty affects people around the world. Twenty-one thousand children a day are dying of malnutrition or preventable disease. They are least able to control their destinies and we are failing them as global citizens. As a society, our priorities are so distorted that we would rather witness the indignity of shoppers fighting over cut-price electrical goods – worked up into a frenzy by the Black Friday pre-Christmas sale hype – than do more to help the starving. Philosophers debate the moral requirement to forgo luxury items for the sake of putting food on children's plates elsewhere, but we would rather add insult to our over-consumptive habits with incivility. Marx penned a wonderful insight: 'The more we find value in external things, the less we find value in ourselves.'

A sign of the problems of our society is the sight of a queue at an empty cash machine, where nobody thinks to tell the person behind them of their frustrated attempt to withdraw money.

Greens say we must redouble our efforts to help those most in need, wherever they live. We need just international institutions that will facilitate the roll-out of medicines and food; and we need state aid buy-in. We must not bite with the other hand, whether by insisting on debt payments which the current generation could have had neither responsibility nor means to pay for, or by engineering markets so that small farmers cannot afford to buy back food to feed their own families which they once could have harvested for themselves, or by treating farmers as just means for acquiring land on which to experiment with GM crops that were refused licences in the EU.

In 2014, I had the honour of meeting Marcus MacFarlane-Barrow, founder of Mary's Meals. His simple idea is to provide one daily meal in places of learning to attract chronically poor children into the classroom and provide them at the same time with a potential route out of poverty. The project started in Malawi and has extended to many other countries. Nearly one million children now benefit. There is something in the simplicity of his plan that puts governments to shame. The 2002 Johannesburg Earth Summit, aimed at combating hunger, poverty and pollution, was notable for its opulence. At a cost of £35 million for 60,000 delegates from 182 countries – including a party of seventy from the UK – champagne and caviar was on the menu, while, on their doorstep, Africa faced a food and water crisis. Perhaps here – not Asda Wembley – a scuffle would have been forgivable.

Future generations are also worthy of our moral consideration. You won't find such a stark reminder of our collective obligations in any other political manifesto. While others obsess about the quarterly financial outlook and current electoral cycle, Greens retain a focus on what we leave behind for generations to come. We know that younger family members will face different challenges to us as adults. Greens want to extend this consideration, to concern ourselves not just with the challenges of the next generation who are already a part of our family but with those of our neighbours and others too, irrespective of whether we know them. And, finally, those generations who aren't around yet but will one day exist, so long as we survive long enough as a species.

The fate of future generations depends on what we do today. How much of a claim should they have on us, though they aren't around yet to ask or insist? The identities of these individuals are not known, and are genetically undetermined, but the fact that such populations will exist is known. Anonymity is no greater a reason to ignore a future person than it is to ignore a person today. The resources of the planet are finite, and not only those whose use is damaging to the environment. John Locke, writing in *The Second Treatise of Government* in 1690, wrote of the appropriation of land as an activity that others had a stake in: 'For he that leaves as much as another can make use of does as good as take nothing at all.' With global population already at seven billion, and set to reach nine billion by 2050, sustainable use of resources is a more acute necessity than it was even in Locke's day, when world population was still under one billion.

OTHER SPECIES

'We do not believe that other species are expendable.'

This is the final claim, concerning the value of inclusivity. The Green Party sets itself apart from other parties by boldly stating its respect for other species. Politics has become so anthropocentric that the absence of such consideration from other party manifestos is rarely noticed. Yet degradation of the planet is sufficiently advanced that we even have our own extinction phase named after us. We do not know exactly how many species inhabit the Earth, since our biological knowledge is incomplete, but even a conservative estimate of a 0.01 per cent extinction rate for 100 million species would mean at least 10,000 species lost each year. This is unprecedented loss. We say it is not just a loss to us but in its own right. A non-speciesist says that other life-forms are not to be judged only in relation to their value to us but also have value in their own right. We think that the individual specimen has a prima facie right to exist – accepting our right to protect ourselves against parasites and other disease-bearing species – and that the fact of extinction is a fact worthy of lament and prevention.

The claim is not that all species are to be given equal weight, as it would be thought wrong to put the life of a non-human animal ahead of that of a human being when both were in danger and only one could be saved. Still, the way in which we treat non-human animals needs urgent attention. We should not be inflicting pain upon our fellow creatures; nor can we treat animals inhumanely when rearing, transporting or killing them for food. Agriculture on an industrial scale has turned livestock into just so many parcels of battery meat, with insufficient attention paid to their distress, suffering or general well-being.

Equality

Our affirmation of the value of inclusivity leads us naturally to the value of equality. After identifying victims of discrimination, the hungry home and abroad, the people of some distant future, or other species and non-human animals as fit and proper subjects of our political consideration, we must then decide upon our political objectives to meet their good. What underpins the fair treatment of ethnic minorities, or of women? What about the satisfaction of the needs of the poor? What of the claims of other species to exist and of animals to humane treatment? At bottom, these are all claims to equality.

Equalities of outcome and opportunity

Equality is about fairness and rights. It's a pretty basic foundational value, but one which Conservatives and Labour seem to have lost all contact with. For us, equality means guaranteeing everybody a minimal set of goods – the ones necessary for the living of a decent life, such as access to health, housing and education – irrespective of ability to pay. Health and housing are measured by outcome, while education is a matter of equality of opportunity and access to resource. We don't say that the market rules or that the postcode lottery should decide who wins and who loses a minimally decent life. We don't barter with your emergency treatment under the pretext of squaring a funding crisis caused largely by the privatisation of health services or the selling of fake financial products in casino-style banks – underwritten by our savings. We don't say it's OK for a council to run down their social housing with the intention of giving it over to developers for demolition and subsequently pricing the evicted community out of any prospect to return there. We don't say it's OK to build a £100 million civic centre – as has happened in Brent, opened in 2013, to be paid for over twenty-five years on debt finance plus interest – while in the same breath closing half the borough's libraries. These libraries were vital centres of learning, with newspapers and computing resources within easy walk for young, old and students alike. Job opportunities were researched, essays completed and horizons broadened there.

Unfortunately, the negative impact of a closure in public service will often be felt disproportionately by a minority community. The effect may not have been intended, but the possibility of indirect discrimination is there nonetheless. In the case of an ethnic minority, for example – already facing institutionalised discrimination as the target of increased incidences of stop-and-search, or less likely to be called to interview than somebody less qualified, simply for carrying an ethnic name – we need to be especially careful not to further diminish their stake in society. The discrimination faced by a minority ethnic woman in the UK today is greater still. As a woman, she is more likely to be made to endure lower pay than her male counterpart for like work.

Equal treatment does not, however, mean that all interests should be given equal importance or entitlement to free expression by society. We do not have to tolerate the views of religious bigots simply because they believe in them. People who purport to find religious backing for homophobic, sexist or other discriminatory views should expect to find their beliefs challenged; if and when they seek to enact those beliefs in ways harmful to others, they should be stopped. Though we do allow an individual to live freely by their beliefs, even when they do so out of ignorance, we draw the line at their harming of others or imposition upon the free exercise of like liberty. We don't tolerate the intolerable. When a believer sets out to proselytise at Speakers' Corner, or preach bigotry and fantasy, he's fair game for ridicule or challenge. In state-sponsored domains, such as schools, much greater vigilance and care is required.

Tackling injustice: you only need to be Green

Everybody has a right to be treated equally; so, too, should everybody take an interest in combating prejudice wherever it occurs. Morality and anti-discrimination is everybody's business. Nobody is a mere bystander; and we remain involved and connected to others even when we don't fall prey to the discrimination that they alone might have to endure. In my inaugural speech as deputy leader in 2014, I articulated this truth: 'You don't have to be black to want to rail against racial prejudice or persecution. You only need to be Green.' I continued with a series of statements about our determination to combat prejudice, regardless of whether we ourselves were members of the targeted groups: whether gay, woman or disabled; young or old; Muslim, Jew or atheist. One needs only to accept that this conviction is common to each case – a determination to confront injustice of all sorts – to be able to accept the conclusion: that a true Green could be relied upon to recognise the principle and then act in such circumstance.

The Green Party says that anybody should be entitled, if not expected, to rise up against injustice, not just those most directly affected by it. This isn't to deny that members of affected groups often possess particular insights that might better equip them to devise strategies to combat the nature of the oppression. Or they simply may want to take greater ownership over the solution. However, in order to get beyond coping strategies, I believe we need to take greater collective ownership of the problems, often structural, which require collective recognition and action. It's also immensely powerful when people not directly affected by a social harm come out to defy the perpetrators of those harms, in an act of solidarity and kinship with the victims.

All political parties need to raise their credibility amongst ethnic minorities, too, by speaking directly to them on matters of their concern. The Green Party is no exception. We need to improve our diversity at all levels of the party, in the membership at large and amongst our elected representatives, in order to look more like the society we purport to represent.

Climate justice

Perhaps the biggest question of our time is: will human beings be able to combat climate change? In the post-industrial era, we have been responsible for unprecedented levels of carbon dioxide emissions through daily production and consumption activities, and especially by the burning of fossil fuels. CO_2 and other gaseous pollutants have accumulated in the atmosphere to a greater extent than before, resulting in heat from the Earth that would otherwise have dissipated getting trapped. Just one consequence of a warmer world is sea-level rise, due to increased volume from ice-melt and thermal expansion of seas. People in coastal areas are already on the sharp end of these negative impacts, and are dying from them. Generally, it is those who were least individually responsible for the problem, and now least able to afford the remedial action to survive, who are being most directly affected. The coastal communities of Bangladesh expend CO_2 at a fraction of the level of Western consumers, person for person. Climate change mitigation is a justice issue, especially the notion that some are being made to suffer the consequences – and suffer them first! – of actions that others were mainly responsible for. Situations don't get much more unequal than that, and lack of proximity does not entitle us to escape the moral consequences of our actions.

It's easy for us to become overwhelmed by the scale of the challenge. We are told there is a tipping point to climate science, a point beyond which there is no return from the trajectory of warming we've set in train. This also takes into account positive feedback loops – where a rise in temperature sets off additional release of methane, which itself contributes to temperature rise, and so on – and the lag between the harmful actions having been taken and the net consequences of those actions. In the 2010 edition of this book, I cited a psychological tendency to pity our own predicament as partially responsible for our own failure to act. Instead, a proper recognition of what's at stake and who is collectively responsible for it should give us all the motivation we need. People don't generally set out to consciously deny responsibility for their actions, but they can end up forming character traits in which they unconsciously do so. These days we have reams of information about the harm we are doing as a species to the biosphere, to other species and to the well-being of those who aren't around yet.

Greens argue that by consuming less, by reducing one's harms to the planet, not only can one continue to live one's life to the full, but one will probably be happier, too. When people act out of a recognition that things have value beyond the satisfaction of consumerist desires – like the growing of one's own food or the repair of a household item – they tend to find greater fulfilment. Our current economic system is part of the problem, not the solution. We need to move towards a method of valuing and bartering things that incorporates a cost to the planet, including the dumping onto the land of playthings that have supposedly expended their shelf-life. Currency is a convention. Dollar bills have the value we choose to give them, over and above their production costs. As things stand, we are pegging the value of a currency to something that distorts the consequences of our activity and facilitates our living in denial. But we could choose to change our idea of currency into something that enhances our appreciation of value and reminds us of the consequences of our actions instead.

A carbon-centred currency can do that. Imagine everybody having a credit card that deducted units of carbon from an annual carbon allowance every time a purchase was made, each weighted according to its environmental impact. Flights wouldn't be prohibited but they would be more costly in terms of carbon spend, and each of us would have to ration our trips accordingly. Quotas of carbon would be distributed equitably and personal savings on the allowance could be treated as net benefits to future generations, as opposed to being sold to the highest bidder.

Means and ends

Over and above inclusivity and equality, Green politics is also about how to set about putting things right. In politics, we often hear the refrain, 'The end doesn't justify the means.' But this doesn't yet tell us what means are conducive to our ends, or permissible in their own right. We know it's wrong to incarcerate people on a remote island – as we have done on Guantanamo since 2003 – against their will and against any kind of humane process. The very act of labelling such prisoners 'illegal combatants' – neither subject to the protections of the Geneva Convention as prisoners of war nor treated as citizens under international human rights legislation – was designed to dehumanise them. Under the pretext of a 'war on terror', the state itself became a terrorist, a direct agent in the kidnap and torture of suspects who were neither charged nor tried. Obama promised to close the prison camp and he, too, let us down. I want to highlight two means identified in our core values, in turn:

Non-violence

'We look for non-violent solutions to conflict situations.'

How can we best respond to conflict situations? Our approach is shaped by a recognition that violence tends to beget violence. If we attempt to impose our will by force, even with justice on our side, there is a real prospect of greater harm resulting and increased numbers of innocents made to suffer and die. We would rather pursue peaceful means of change. That means talk, negotiation and the application of international pressure through consensus building. None of this is the stuff of Hollywood actioners – where violence is glorified or glamorised – but it can be shown to work in the long-run, and more reliably than war.

Our leaders betray failure of imagination on a grand scale when they resort to war without exhausting all peaceable routes. The well intentioned may also be acting out of bad faith, whether from consideration for domestic popularity or hubristic pretensions of grandeur. Would that we could arrange for all the demagogues and warmongers of the world to act out their campaigns of violence in controlled environments, preferably virtual ones, out of the way of the rest of us!

Violent conflict may sometimes by unavoidable or necessary, but it must be a last resort and proportionate in object and means. Few wars waged by Western governments in recent decades meet these criteria, especially in the Middle East. When leaders say, 'We cannot but act! Now!' we should be especially critical. Engaging in violent conflict is not the only way of acting, yet the false assumption is often made that stopping short of that is bound to be ineffective.

If our goal is peace, then isn't the practice of non-violence going to be more conducive to that end? Shouldn't the aim itself constrain us in what means we may adopt to bring it about? A critical, enlightened notion inspired by the teachings of Gandhi is that 'the means are the ends in the making'. We can be judged both for the quality of what we aim for and the quality of how we aim. There is a value both in the goal and in how we choose to obtain it. Generally, the value of the goal gives us a clue as to the means that we should use to reach it. Justice clearly has this character, as both an outcome to be desired and a means by which that outcome is constrained. The use of information acquired through torture of a suspect, for example, would defeat the very object of the trial. Injustice cannot coexist with justice. Nor can we justify indiscriminate air strikes resulting in the deaths of the very people we claimed to be acting on behalf of – killing them in order to save them?

Campaigning politics

'Electoral politics is not the only way to achieve change in society.'

Non-violence is key also to campaigns to overturn bad laws or harmful practices. When, in 1955 Alabama, Rosa Parks refused to cede to a racist request to give up her seat on a bus, she helped inspire a civil rights movement. In 2014, Greens continue to be great practitioners of this method. Caroline Lucas was arrested for peaceful protest against fracking. Jenny Jones was arrested, then promptly 'de-arrested', for peaceful protest in Parliament Square, alongside others in the Occupy movement. Action speaks louder than words alone, especially when non-violent.

Greens have a tendency to punch above their weight and that's not just because we went into politics for the right reasons, but owing to a recognition that politics goes wider than electoral politics. Career politicians we are not, and professionalisation of the party can only get us so far, at risk of subverting our vitality. I sometimes joke with new members that one doesn't go into Green politics to get elected quickly, or even at all. That's because our motivation extends to politics all around and every day. Just look at how much injustice happens in daily life: do we walk by or do we intervene?

I have always been political. For as long as I've been able to think for myself, I've been bothered about why there should be conflict in the world, what we can do to collectively address global poverty, and why people should be treated fairly.

My concern is hardly professional: it is human. In the beginning, my thoughts may have been punctuated by surprise. As my knowledge of the world has grown, something akin persists: incredulity. I am incredulous that we cannot arrange human affairs better than this. With all our ingenuity, it cannot be beyond the wit of human person to see through the short-termism of our age; we are losing sight of the value of the things that really matter, from the inescapable beauty of our natural world and the legacy we leave behind to the avoidable deaths of starving human populations and our mistreatment of farmed animals.

I regularly show up at election counts for public elections that I or comrades have stood in. I think I've found that the crosses on our ballot papers are more often assertively marked than for the other parties! I'm left with a sense that our voters both know what we stand for and realise that we are the best hope for a better future.

This book is an attempt from within the Green Party to demonstrate that conviction and the reasons why you should vote Green.

Chapter 2

Climate Change

DAVID FLINT

We need to act now to avoid the worst consequences of climate change, for those consequences would be a catastrophe for our civilisation and our species – and for many other species too. Climate change is the most serious threat we face – much more dangerous than Ebola or terrorism.

Fortunately, we know what we have to do and it is possible. We also know that the side effects of doing it will be good for most of the world's people – 99 per cent or more will gain improved health and well-being.

Only the Greens truly understand the problem and only the Greens are determined to fix it. If climate change is high on your agenda and if you want an evidence-based approach to our future, you should vote Green.

Major threat

The work of the Inter-governmental Panel on Climate Change (IPCC) is probably the largest and most rigorous examination of a scientific issue ever. That work has continued for twenty-eight years, has produced a series of authoritative reports and was recognised by the Nobel Prize for Peace in 2007. The most recent report of 2014 – the work of 830 scientists – concluded: 'Continued emission of greenhouse gases will … [increase] the likelihood of *severe, pervasive and irreversible impacts* for people and ecosystems.'

Climate change will degrade the environment, drive species to extinction, reduce food production, destroy lives and livelihoods and increase migration.

The greenhouse gases (GHGs) that we emit in our everyday lives, and which are emitted by farms and factories in supporting those lives, have already caused such changes. Nothing can now prevent more change, since the momentum is already present in the climate system.

Temperature rise	Degrees
To date	0.75
Now inevitable	1.5
At which catastrophic changes are more likely than not	2.0
Likely by 2050 if we carry on as we are	1.9

If we continue to emit greenhouse gases at the current rate then we will reach the point of catastrophic change by the middle of this century.

Primer on climate change

At its most basic level, the sun warms the Earth and greenhouse gases block the loss of some of that heat to space, causing the sea and land to grow warmer. The main greenhouse gas is carbon dioxide, which is produced when we burn coal, wood, oil, gas and other fuels. It's also produced as a by-product of certain industrial processes, notably cement production. Methane, another important greenhouse gas, is released by rotting vegetation and as a by-product of the digestive processes of cows, i.e. as cow belches.

The seas and forests naturally absorb these gases without harm provided the quantities are not too great. The quantities first became too great in about 1920 and have increased substantially since then. In addition, we have reduced the area of forest available to absorb the gases. Atmospheric CO_2 has risen continuously since then. In 1987, it exceeded 350 parts per million (ppm) for the first time in at least 800,000 years. In April 2014, it exceeded 400 ppm for the first time and stayed above 400 for three months.[1]

The main drivers for these sustained yet unsustainable increases are the growth in the numbers and prosperity of the human species. In the last 150 years, hundreds of millions have escaped from poverty to enjoy lives unimagined by our ancestors; lives in which leisure, travel and meat are commonplace while hunger, illness and fear are rare. But the increasing levels of atmospheric greenhouse gases make the planet warmer, raise sea levels and make the sea more acidic, and the more gases there are, the greater the effect.

Environmental degradation

Climate change is already producing visible changes. It has:

- Increased global air and sea temperatures by about 0.85°C so far
- Raised sea level at 2 mm per annum
- Reduced the summer volume of Arctic ice by 62 per cent since 1980[2]
- Caused most glaciers to shrink significantly
- Increased the acidity of the seas by 26 per cent[3]
- Increased the frequency of heatwaves, droughts and heavy downpours

---

1   National Oceanic and Atmospheric Administration, 2014.
2   Polar Science Centre, 2014.
3   Intergovernmental Panel on Climate Change.

If we continue to emit GHGs at the present rate – the business-as-usual scenario – we may expect by 2100:

- A temperature rise of 3–5.5°C[4]
- A sea-level rise of 60 to 95 cm
- Further shrinkage in glaciers, with a volume loss up to 85 per cent
- Much more extreme weather

We also expect several 'positive feedback' effects to kick in. Here are two:

- Higher temperatures will cause even faster loss of the Arctic ice. Since open water absorbs four times as much sunlight as ice, the rate of Arctic warming will be increased.
- Right across the lands next to the higher temperatures, permafrost will melt (permafrost is frost that never melts – until now) releasing methane from rotting vegetation that has been trapped under the frost.

The quantities of methane are very uncertain but might be comparable in climatic effect to the total amount of CO_2 released so far. Therefore the effects of climate change could be much worse than current IPCC projections. They are unlikely to be better.

Species extinction

Many species are threatened by loss of habitat; pesticide use, poaching and climate change will add to the pressures. According to the IPCC, 'A large fraction of species face increased extinction risk due to climate change during and beyond the twenty-first century.'

---

4   Intergovernmental Panel on Climate Change.

As temperatures increase, many species will need to move, generally away from the equator or to higher ground, to find a suitable habitat. Most plants, small mammals and freshwater molluscs will be unable to move fast enough. Others will find their movements blocked by rivers, mountains or other natural features or by human fences and settlements. In addition, marine organisms will suffer from reduced oxygen and increased acidification.

Reduced food production

Climate change is likely to reduce food production after 2030. Droughts, storms and higher temperatures will reduce yields while rising sea levels will reduce the area under cultivation, according to the IPCC.

Of course, it's very likely that the rest of this century will see better crop varieties and farming methods, which will tend to increase yields. Unfortunately, this effect must be set against both the increasing demand for food, and especially for meat, from major developing countries like India and China and the land used for crops grown to produce biofuels, as well as the damage done by climate change. It's very unlikely that it can do all of that.[5]

The most likely long-term outcome will be increased demand and stagnant production, leading to increased competition and higher prices. Inevitably, the main losers will be the poorest people.

Effect on lives

Climate change will be – already is – deadly. The European heatwave of 2003 is estimated to have killed 70,000 people.[6] For the Somalian

---

5   Ray, D. K., Mueller, N. D., West, P. C., Foley, J. A. (19 June 2013) 'Yield Trends Are Insufficient to Double Global Crop Production by 2050', PLOS ONE 8 (6): e66428. doi:10.1371/journal.pone.0066428.

6   Robine, J. M. et al., 'Death toll exceeded 70,000 in Europe during the summer of 2003', *C. R. Biol.*, vol. 331, no. 2 (2008), pp. 171–8.

famine of 2010 to 2012, the estimate is 260,000. Though neither was
due solely to climate change, they were both made more likely by it
– and they show two aspects of a hotter world.

In the north of Kenya we see another example. Here the desert
has expanded at the expense of pasture – and the pasture at the
expense of cropland. Many herders and farmers have left their families to seek work in the cities. Around the world there are many
other communities whose way of life, and even survival, is threatened by climate change.

What will happen to the people as the seas rise, the glaciers
retreat and deserts spread? Many, of course, will starve. Others will
try to move but, like the endangered species, will often find their
paths blocked by natural or man-made obstacles, such as national
borders.

What happens next is beyond sensible prediction, but illegal
migration and massive refugee camps are inevitable. As tensions
rise – often reinforced by national and religious differences – wars
for water and land are bound to follow. Some, at least, will occur in
and around existing conflicts such as Palestine, Iraq, Afghanistan and
Kashmir. It's sobering to remember that both sides in the Kashmir
dispute possess nuclear weapons. Even without nuclear war, some
weak states may collapse – as Somalia did after 1991.

Effect on UK

Climate change will be bad for the UK too. One lesson of winter
2013/14 is that we need to sharply increase what we spend on
flood defences. The other effects of climate change will clearly
demand additional spending on defence, amelioration and compensation. Some important wetlands will be lost to the sea, together
with the birds and other animals that live there. It will also dis-
rupt the lifecycles of a variety of animals, in ways that are largely
unpredictable.

The UK cannot feed its population from its own resources and must therefore import food. Rising food prices will make this progressively more expensive and some favourite foods, such as coffee and chocolate, may become very expensive. The UK government has seen climate change as a threat to UK national security for some years. In 2008, the National Security Strategy said that 'climate change is potentially the greatest challenge to global stability and security, and therefore to national security', and went on to contemplate more frequent territorial disputes and intense humanitarian crises.[7]

We may also expect repeated rounds of panic over immigration. If it follows recent precedent, the government of the day will respond to these real and supposed threats by pandering to prejudice, increasing controls, reducing civil liberties and refusing to examine the real causes. As financial and environmental pressures increase, we should expect a decline in goodwill and compassion in both politics and the population generally. The recent rise of UKIP gives us a taste of what that may look like. Those of us who remember the rise of the National Front in the 1970s will fear what may follow.

A moral issue

It's important to stress that, for Greens, climate change is a *moral* issue. Greens believe that humanity does not own the Earth. We are, at most, its stewards for our time. We do not have the right to destroy the rainforest, drive species to extinction and impose the costs of coping with climate change on future generations. There is a moral obligation on all peoples, countries and corporations to live sustainably, to stop this rape of the Earth. To meet this obligation we should ensure that global temperatures do not rise by more than 1.5 degrees. This is now effectively impossible so we accept, reluctantly, a target of 2 degrees.

---

7   'The National Security Strategy of the United Kingdom: Security in an interdependent world', Cabinet Office, 2008.

UK's position

The UK's obligation is particularly onerous. The UK started the industrial revolution by burning coal and our prosperity is still based on burning coal – both here and in countries that make goods for us. Yet most of the costs of climate change fall on much poorer countries. On Bangladesh, for instance – 10 per cent of which is less than 1 metre above sea level. Or on Somalia, which has endured many years of anthropogenic drought and famine.

The Green Party believes that we have no right to flood poor countries and create droughts across the tropics while displacing indigenous people so that our companies can exploit their oil and palm trees. We also believe that we, along with other developed countries, owe the victims our best efforts to avert the climate problems, our help in addressing those that are not averted and compensation for the damage we do. Specifically, the UK should reduce its GHG emissions faster than the world as a whole.

In addressing climate change, as in many other policy areas, only the Greens stand for the poor, the future and the rest of the natural world. To avoid catastrophic climate change will require a profound economic transformation but one that our experience between 1939 and 1945 shows is possible.

Here are some of the key changes we need:

DECARBONISE THE ENERGY SYSTEM

In 2013, 86 per cent of the UK's energy came from fossil fuels, mainly coal, oil and gas, 47 per cent of which was imported.[8] Our dependence on energy imports has two major disadvantages: it makes it harder to ensure continuity of supply, i.e. keeping the lights on, and it makes it difficult to criticise aggression and human rights abuses by our suppliers – Russia and Saudi Arabia are just the current examples.

We need to replace our fossil fuel stations with low-carbon power

---

8   MacLeay, Iain, Harris, Kevin, Annut, Anwar et al. (2014) 'Digest of United Kingdom Energy Statistics 2014', Department of Energy and Climate Change.

sources such as hydro, solar, tidal power and wind. Nuclear power is also low-carbon, but continued connections with the UK's nuclear weapons programme, uncertainties over waste disposal, high costs and the lack of commercial insurance all confirm Greens' long-standing hostility to nuclear power.

ELECTRIFY TRANSPORT

In the UK, transport was responsible for 21 per cent of GHG emissions in 2012. We can cut this by completing the electrification of the railways, encouraging people to switch from cars to public transport or bikes, replacing diesel buses with trams and hybrid engines, and using electric cars, as well as moving to more energy-efficient vehicles generally.

REDUCE WASTE OF ENERGY

A lot of energy is wasted due to the use of inefficient machines and a lack of care by users. We can and should switch to more efficient machines. There's a general need for every business and every household to review its energy use. Most will find much inefficiency – improperly maintained machines, lights left on etc. – which can be eliminated over time. In some cases the need is for a change in the fundamental technology, e.g. from incandescent bulbs to LEDs or, as George Monbiot has argued in *Heat* (2006), from Portland cement to geopolymeric cement.

The biggest single source of energy waste is that for inefficient space heating of buildings. In 2009, about 16 per cent of the UK's GHG emissions were due to space heating.[9] Since the energy inefficiency of British buildings is notorious and since the best buildings use 90 per cent less energy than average ones, we could make major savings by improving our stock of buildings.

To address this, Greens would use a mixture of regulations, grants

---

9   Emissions from Heat, Statistical Summary, Department of Energy and Climate Change, 2012.

and incentives. For instance, we would introduce regulations setting much higher efficiency standards for houses, cars and household appliances. We would require landlords to achieve high energy performance standards before their properties could be let. We would also improve and expand existing schemes that make the necessary improvements affordable.

REDUCE WASTE

A great deal of the world's energy is consumed, largely in developing countries like China, in making things for use in countries like ours. No wonder the Chinese smell hypocrisy in our demands that they cut their greenhouse gas emissions! But we do need to cut those emissions and we should do it by wasting less. From a green perspective, it is wasteful to throw away a coat or a phone or a chair that is still usable just because a better or more fashionable one is now available.

Greens seek to change attitudes, to encourage people to value quality above fashion. We want people to buy less but better stuff. When they have finished with stuff then we favour reuse through formal sharing systems such as Freegle, selling at car boot sales or on eBay, or just by giving to friends or charity shops. Only if none of those is suitable do we favour recycling. This focus on buying less stuff is one of our most radical policies, since it aims at a reduction in goods bought – and therefore almost certainly in GDP. To the dominant Western religion – growthism – it is an evil heresy. Yet it is essential if we are to meet our emissions targets. It will also reduce our consumption of raw materials such as metals, the prices of which have been rising for the last decade.

LESS INTENSIVE AGRICULTURE

Western agriculture is strongly dependent on fossil fuels which are used in cultivation, transport and in the manufacture of the many chemicals used in modern agriculture. Globally, however, the biggest agriculture emissions come from deforestation and as a by-product of meat production. We need the forests both for the many species that find their homes in them and to absorb some of our emissions.

These policies amount to a fundamental transformation of both economy and lifestyles. Instead of worshipping growth as the solution to all social problems, we must see the economy as the way to meet our material needs with the least impact on the environment and other species. A new green economy will provide many new opportunities and jobs. Under the Green New Deal, many new jobs will be created in public transport, renewable energy and building improvement.[10] Many of these will be publicly funded but there will be scope for entrepreneurs as well, especially in energy systems.

STRONG GOVERNMENT POLICIES

Government must set the strategy, because most businesses do not think sufficiently long-term. It must also act directly by planning, organising and funding adaptation measures such as flood defences. But as we are not a command economy, government also needs to motivate people and businesses to act and to help them do the right things.

HIGH EFFICIENCY STANDARDS

Government already sets and even enforces safety and efficiency standards in many sectors. The building regulations, to take a critical example, set standards for home insulation. The current standards are welcome, but inadequate houses and flats last many decades – many of us live in homes that were built in Victoria's reign! Therefore, we ought to be building houses that are fit for the conditions – climatic and economic – that will apply in fifty years' time. Specifically, they need to be fit for a warmer world in which greenhouse gas emissions have become much less acceptable.

---

10   www.europeangreens.eu/content/green-new-deal, accessed 9 January 2015.

The same principles apply to power stations. If a station will last thirty years it should be built to meet emissions requirements of 2045. No actual or planned fossil fuel power station can meet this requirement. It's possible that gas-fired stations that capture and bury the CO_2 emitted will meet this standard in the future. We would fund research on this but not rely on its working effectively.

The easiest way to reduce fossil fuel use is to make it more expensive. A Green government would achieve this by imposing carbon taxes on all such fuels. To avoid penalising the poor, the Green Party would introduce a citizen's income as part of a root-and-branch reform of our appalling welfare system.

One necessary consequence – in fact, the key purpose – of carbon taxes and other policies will be to ensure that most fossil fuel reserves are left in the ground. And that will reduce the economic power of the corporations and countries that control fossil fuels.

HALT HABITAT DESTRUCTION

The main responsibility for stopping the loss of habitats such as rainforests must lie with the countries that have them. A Green UK government would offer technical assistance to these countries and would ban the import of any forest products that had not been produced sustainably.

REDUCE POWER OF CAPITAL

Many of our policies will be very unwelcome to major corporations. Greens know this and would take steps to reduce their political power. This power has increased markedly in recent decades, to the point where some are able to sue governments in private courts for such 'offences' as banning nuclear power and protecting their citizens from cancer! We would regulate lobbying and reform electoral finance.

REDUCE INEQUALITY

For the last thirty years, corporations, their managers and apologists

have defended increasing inequality as the necessary means to produce the growth that would make us all richer. No ideology is needed
to see that this has not worked. 'Saving the planet' means an end to
growth – at least of material stuff. A Green government would therefore take steps to reduce inequality both by raising the incomes of
the poor and limiting those of the rich.

Only the Green Party stands for these policies

And so we see that preventing catastrophic climate change requires
more than a series of technical fixes. More, even, than a new energy
system. It requires a transformation of politics and of society. This
will be hugely challenging. It will require a bold government with
a strong mandate. Only the Green Party has the policies to save us
from disaster and only a Green government would implement them.

Yet there's good news too. For, even apart from avoiding catastrophic climate change, these changes will be highly beneficial to
everyone. The society we want has the benefits of better jobs, better health, less crime and more time for family and the community.
Here's how...

BETTER HEALTH

Poor health is not only damaging to the individual, it is a loss to society and a cost to the NHS. Most climate change mitigation policies
have large health benefits.[11] For instance:

- When we walk and cycle more and take more physical exercise
  we enjoy the better health and fitness that follows.
- Stopping the burning of fossil fuels, especially coal, will cut bad
  health due to air pollution.
- Reductions in the use of fossil fuels, especially diesel, for

11   Flint, David (2013): 'How "saving the planet" will improve our health', Green Econom-
     ics Institute.

transport will also improve air quality. Poor air quality is estimated to cost 35,000 lives per year in the UK alone.

- Reducing inequality will reduce obesity, drug abuse, mental illness and infant mortality.[12]

LESS CRIME

There is strong evidence that more unequal societies are more violent. According to the Equality Trust, '[Even] small permanent decreases in inequality – such as reducing inequality from the level found in Spain to that in Canada – would reduce homicides by 20 per cent and lead to a 23 per cent long-term reduction in robberies.' A lower crime rate has many benefits to health, welfare and public finances.

MORE TIME FOR FAMILY AND COMMUNITY

A Greener society would have a quite different work/life balance from today's. On the one hand, people would be less acquisitive, less greedy, would buy less and be less fashion conscious. These changes in consumer behaviour would require businesses to focus less on fashion and more on quality. Therefore, they would change more slowly and cease to demand unreasonably long hours.

And Green policies for secure employment would be more acceptable to employers if their markets changed more slowly. The shorter and more predictable hours will give people more time for family and community. This is something that everyone claims to want but which grey-party governments have shown themselves unwilling to provide.

WELL-BEING AS GOAL OF POLICY

Thus, the actions needed to avert catastrophic climate change will improve our health and well-being substantially. Most political parties say that they want to see increases in health and well-being. But

---

12 Wilkinson, Richard, and Pickett, Kate (2010): *The Spirit Level: Why Equality is Better for Everyone.*

it's clear that they will never give health and well-being priority over their quasi-religious commitment to economic growth. Two examples will suffice to show this: roads have been engineered to exclude pedestrians, making them too dangerous for many children to walk to school; and action on alcohol pricing and food labelling has been blocked by commercial lobbying.

Only Greens, with their commitment to human values and evidence-based policy, will follow through on their commitments. We are, in fact, extraordinarily lucky that we do not have to choose between saving the climate and improving people's lives. It might easily have been different.

Climate change mitigation will not solve all our social problems. Greens recognise the need for new approaches to social as well as environmental problems. But, more than any other issue, tackling climate change will set us on the path to a better future.

If you want to see real progress toward a better society, if you have seen through the false religion of growthism, then you need to vote Green in 2015 and in the years to come.

David Flint is chairman of Enfield Green Party and parliamentary candidate for Enfield North. He used to be a management consultant and researcher and is now a visiting fellow at the Cass Business School. @enfield_greens

Chapter 3

Economy

MOLLY SCOTT CATO

A Green revolution in the economy

Whether or not the Green approach to economic policy might persuade you to vote Green really depends on what you think an economy is for. Conventional wisdom is that the economy's primary design feature should be to grow. Slow growth is greeted with a sense of doom whereas rapid growth is celebrated. This focus on the quantity rather than the quality of the economy is challenged by Greens, who are seeking to re-evaluate our relationship with the planet we share with seven billion other humans and millions of other species. When seen from this perspective, an economy growing out of control is less cause for celebration and more a demand for urgent change. This leads us to think differently about how we use the abundant natural resources the planet makes available and how the economic value we can generate with them is shared.

Demanding less and sharing more

One thing most people know about green economics is that Greens do not share the ubiquitous idea that size matters beyond all else. Not only are we fond of the mantra that 'small is beautiful' but we also reject the idea that growth of the economy is necessarily a good thing. It seems obvious that, if the limits of our planet are fixed, then at some point the economy must stop growing. Bizarrely, this is disputed by conventional economists, who argue that ingenuity can always find a way for us to get more from less, by greater efficiency and substitution of one resource for another. While Greens are committed to efficient use of resources and energy and to technological innovations to facilitate these, we challenge the idea that economic growth can continue forever within the confines of a limited planet.

We would go further and argue that the problems of pollution, the disruption of the natural balance of the carbon and nitrogen cycles, and the extinction of species are all indicators that our economy has already reached the safety limits and that we are, in an ecological sense, living beyond our means. This is an infinitely more serious conclusion than the idea that we are living beyond our means financially. After all, money is a human creation, something we can control if the political will is there. Nature is a power beyond our control, whose complex systems and feedback loops we are still struggling to understand. The first lesson of green economics is that we need to get our thinking straight on what really matters, and this isn't about the economy, stupid.

Beyond the question of whether growth on the current exponential pattern is sustainable, we can also question whether economic growth is bringing us the benefits it promises. Green economist Richard Douthwaite wrote a ground-breaking book more than two decades ago called *The Growth Illusion* which challenged this myth. The book's subtitle is telling: 'How growth has enriched the few, impoverished the many and endangered the planet'. He provided evidence that once economies exceed a certain size and complexity, they no longer increase human happiness because the cost to social and ecological systems starts generating negative consequences such as pollution, crime, mental illness and so on. He argued that we should be looking to determine the optimal size of the economy and focus more on resilient local economies rather than thrusting, competitive national ones.

If we follow the trajectory of life in post-war Britain we can grasp the human side of his argument. Directly after the war, economic growth was necessary to replace the infrastructure destroyed by six long years of bombing and fighting, and to reconstruct civilian systems to replace the military ones. The frugality of the 1950s gave way to the early consumerism of the 1960s, a time remembered as a heyday of social and cultural flourishing. But the pressure to grow continued through the 1970s, with the emphasis on the stimulus of consumer demand, whether through innovative gadgetry, built-in obsolescence or the need to keep up with rapidly changing fashion. Shopping was gradually transformed from being a rare treat to an oppressive national duty. Throughout this period and up to the present day, we moved from an economy that comfortably met our need to a bloated one that increased our stress levels and damaged our natural environment.

Economic justice within and between countries

Economic growth has traditionally been used as a way of deflecting demands for fair shares: since your portion of pie is larger than last year why should you protest that the slice of the financier or property developer is growing much more rapidly? But once growth stops, the question of how we share out the pie becomes a much more urgent one. This is why the demand for social justice lies right at the heart of a green approach to economics. It is why we insist on a minimum wage that is also a living wage. It is why we are fighting for tax justice, so that tax becomes the contribution everybody makes to living in a civilised society, not something that is just for little people while the elites and the mighty corporations they control hide their money offshore and laugh at the rest of us. It is why we challenge the global system labelled as 'free' but which is really controlled by the same powerful interests and takes a destructive free ride on the global environment.

The fight over inequality is central to an understanding of how our economy works and what our political priorities should be. Politicians on the right – a prominent example is Boris Johnson – argue that inequality is not only necessary but good. It provides the spur to effort and innovation. Social epidemiologists Wilkinson and Pickett, by contrast, provide evidence of all the ways that inequality damages society, showing that a whole range of social indicators, from teenage pregnancies to drug use and crime, are higher in more unequal societies. Interestingly, the wealthy also do less well in societies where the gap between richest and poorest is higher, suggesting that inequality is fundamentally destructive for us all.

But Greens do not only seek equality in terms of income, we also argue that people should have equality in their workplace. So we favour enterprises organised as co-operatives, where everybody in the firm has a say over how it is managed and people are allowed to have autonomy in their work. This not only provides them with self-confidence and job satisfaction but the skills of self-management spill over into wider society, creating more capable and engaged citizens. An example of a sector where the co-operative model is thriving is renewable energy generation. This is particularly so in Denmark and Germany, where governments including or influenced by Greens have established powerful incentives. Denmark is now able to provide 100 per cent of its electricity from renewable sources at some times in the year and much of this is owned by communities. Similarly, in Germany, the number of renewable energy co-operatives doubled between 2010 and 2013. We are beginning to see similar developments in the UK, where community-owned generation of electricity is increasing rapidly as a response to the wasteful and exploitative domination of the large energy corporations.

The co-operative form of economic organisation ensures that the value produced through economic activity is shared fairly between all those who created it. Another way that firms can contribute to the greater good is through the payment of taxes. These contributions pay for infrastructure such as roads and broadband networks that the companies themselves use. But, over the past several decades, larger corporations have established complex multinational structures which they can use to shift profits around so as to minimise the rate of tax that they pay. They have also done secret deals with national governments to reduce their tax contribution and have used these deals to put pressure on other governments to reduce rates of corporation tax even more.

These beggar-thy-neighbour policies have resulted in a situation where governments can no longer afford to maintain infrastructure or adequately fund public services, which has begun to undermine the economy itself. Amazon has famously avoided paying tax yet it is partly responsible for the damage to roads that its tax would have paid to repair. It declared only €28.8 million of net profit from the €15.5 billion generated in earnings in the EU in 2013. Through basing itself in Luxembourg and transferring payments to other parts of its parent company it avoided much of the tax owing.[13] It also relies on publicly provided health and education services for its workers but is avoiding making an adequate contribution to fund these.

Such corporate tax avoidance is also destroying genuine competition. Imagine a high street in a small town near you that has a locally owned bookshop and café and a branch of Starbucks. The café cannot compete with Starbucks because of the way Starbucks can use its low rate of tax to subsidise the price of its coffee.[14] The bookshop pays tax and cannot compete with Amazon, which can charge lower prices because it does not pay enough tax. So the multinational web of corporate tax avoidance is destroying our

13   http://online.wsj.com/articles/the-amazon-tax-deal-the-eu-is-probing-1413949580, accessed 12 December 2014.
14   http://euranetplus-inside.eu/eu-commission-starbucks-received-illegal-dutch-state-aid, accessed 12 December 2014.

local economies as well as undermining our infrastructure and public services.

Greens are the most active of all the parties on proposing policies for tax justice. We call for transparency in financial reporting, so that tax authorities can know how much money companies make on their territory. This will end the farce of offices in Luxembourg or the Cayman Islands where thousands of companies are registered but no economic activity takes place. We also need to know who gains value (or is the 'beneficial owner') of every company, so that individuals cannot hide behind complex structures of trusts and shell companies. And we need minimum rates of corporate taxation across the single market of the EU to end the corporate tax shopping and tax competition between member states.

The global domination of corporations is highly damaging to the nations of the global south, who are even less equipped to ensure that companies contribute an adequate share of the profits they generate in their territories. Political corruption is often cited as a reason for the continuing poverty of countries like Nigeria or Congo, which have vast natural resources. But a corrupt deal has two parties and the other side of the coin is the irresponsible and unethical behaviour of multinational corporations. It has been estimated that, because of the system of offshore finance, the countries of the south may lose as much as $100 billion in unpaid tax[15] and have been deprived of ten times as much money in taxation due as they have received in aid payments from the wealthier nations.[16]

Thinking differently about resources

Given the importance Greens place on the planet and its precious resources, it is unsurprising that we have a particular approach to

---

15   www.theguardian.com/sustainable-business/2014/nov/03/developing-nations-lose-100bn-tax-revenue-g20-reforms-avoidance, accessed 12 December 2014.

16   Nicholas Shaxson, *Treasure Islands* (2011).

defining and sharing them. It is a crucial difference between a socialist and green approach to economics that the former would demand
the right to work whereas the latter would demand a fair share of
resources. Unlike traditional socialist parties, Greens are less likely
to be found marching for the right to work or for an increase in their
wages and more likely to be found demanding their share of both the
capital and the land that make production possible. In a green economy, the matter of creating wealth should not be left to a class who,
by luck or design, have come to control factories or farms. Rather, we
should all be involved in wealth generation and – whether through
a locally owned wind turbine or a community farm – we should all
have a fair share in the proceeds of that wealth.

As a green economist, I consider the most important resource to
be the land. Although in our fantasies of the weightless economy
and the virtual society many of us have become totally disconnected
from our roots in the land, it remains the case that land is fundamental in providing us with food and other resources necessary to
produce the clothes and gadgets that we set so much store by. The
land is also essential in maintaining clean air and clean water, without which we simply cannot live.

Given the vital importance of land, we need to question particularly how it is shared. The current distribution of land ownership is
illogical, anachronistic and the origin of much of the inequity that
characterises the global economy. In some ways this is even truer
in Europe than in the countries of the world where people are still
struggling for their land rights. We have forgotten that we are poor
because we were thrown off our land so that we now have to sell
our labour to survive and pay rent to somebody whose right to own
property costs us a sizeable share of our income on a monthly basis.

To resolve the problem of land ownership generating inequality,
Greens would introduce a land value tax. This would be a charge on
the rentable value of all land that reflects its usefulness and repre-
sents a price the owner should pay to the community for the privilege

of ownership. In an urban context, land value tax could replace the council tax, which would be similar to adding additional bands at the top of the current range. But land value tax would also be charged on development land, so that the increased value of that land when planning permission was granted could be shared amongst the community as a whole rather than being the exclusive preserve of the property developer. And the tax would also be charged on agricultural land, ending the medieval system of landed estates that lie beyond the reach of economic policy but maintain a system of privilege and hierarchy that has no place in the twenty-first century.

Those who own land have traditionally been able to exist without working, since they have been able to charge rents on their property and live from the proceeds. Greens think this is unfair and inefficient. But, by introducing a charge on property ownership, we could generate enough income to fund a payment to all citizens, known as a citizen's income. This would not be a vast payment but it would be enough to meet basic needs, freeing people from the obligation to take poor-quality low-pay employment and removing the fear of destitution.

Emancipating the money system

Unlike our key European neighbours, France and Germany, the British islands are not hugely endowed with resources and so, like the younger brother who has little to inherit, we have learnt to live by our wits. We have been ingenious, historically in design and manufacturing and, more recently, in the field of finance. From the perspective of the real economy – and particularly given Green concerns about equality – the move from structural to financial engineering has not been a positive one for the UK or for the global economy.

The first many people knew about the complex financial 'instruments' that really amount to little more than risk-taking and gambling was when the financial crisis hit and we realised that we, as the public of democratic nations, were guaranteeing these risks.

The vast financial and economic cost has yet to be measured since we are still all struggling with huge public debts incurred through bailing out banks, while the real economy of factories, offices and shops is still suffering from the reductions in wages and weak investment that followed the financial crisis.

There are also serious, negative consequences of an economy that focuses so heavily on finance. Speculative investments receive much higher returns than investments in productive activity in the real economy. This leads to what economists call 'crowding out', where money cannot be raised for useful investments – in green infrastructure, for example – because it has been sucked into worthless, purely financial investments. For this reason, and because of their inherent risk, Greens would severely curtail the activities that financial corporations are legally permitted to engage in and would require all financial 'products' to pass a social usefulness test before being licensed.[17]

The Green Party is also critical of the way money is currently created, with a parallel creation of debts and in the private sector, meaning that the banks, a particular form of private corporation, have a vast and unaccountable power to decide what is and is not funded in our economy. Our policy is to move towards a form of public credit creation, enabling the government to fund public services and projects without the need to incur crippling debts and to pay interest to people whose only contribution is the ownership of capital.

Conclusion

There is a consistency across all the different aspects of what might broadly be called economic policy, and that is the habit Greens have of challenging fundamental assumptions not just about how wealth

---

17   See the Green Party report 'Stepping Outside the Casino', http://greenparty.org.uk/ files/peoplepic/Natalie%20Bennett/FINALbankingreport.pdf, accessed 12 December 2014.

is distributed but about how it is produced and how the resources that enable its production are owned and used. This grows quite naturally out of our somewhat trite but still serviceable slogan that we should have a politics for people and planet. Since the planet is the source of all wealth, we have a right to demand assets rather than accepting the contract of wage slavery. But our demands must be tempered by our understanding that we have only one planet and we have to learn to live within its limits. This is not a remedy that suggests a grim future huddling around a candle wearing an itchy hair-shirt. Rather, it requires us to question what we really value and to replace the tawdry consumerism that we live with today with a richer society based in vibrant communities with strong local economies and fulfilling human relationships.

Molly Scott Cato is a Green MEP. Before that, she was a Professor of Green Economics. She wrote the book Green Economics *and has published widely in academic journals and popular media. @MollyMEP*

Chapter 4

Education

MARTIN FRANCIS

Teachers are oppressed by a huge workload that feels unrelated to the real needs of children, whose natural curiosity and creativity is stifled by lessons geared towards passing tests, and parents who fear their children are being robbed of their childhood. Those are the issues the Green Party feels passionately about and wants to change.

A key Green Party core value states: 'The success of a society cannot be measured by narrow economic indicators, but should take account of factors affecting the quality of life for all people: personal freedom, social equity, health, happiness and human fulfilment.'

The Green Party's education policy reflects that value, which immediately puts it on a collision course with what has become known as the Global Education Reform Movement – otherwise known as the GERM.[18]

The GERM

Pasi Sahlberg, who coined the phrase, lists five features of the GERM:

Standardisation of education based on easily measured outcomes

---

18   www.pasisahlberg.com/text-test, accessed 12 December 2014.

enforced by testing, league tables and performance-related pay for teachers.

Focus on core subjects of reading, writing, mathematics and science, which are used to set targets and become indices of international competiveness via Pisa tables and similar measures.

The search for low-risk ways of achieving these goals, which involve teaching to the test and a narrow definition of curriculum, teaching and learning.

The use of corporate management models with policies linked to economic rather than moral goals.

Test-based accountability, which means schools and individual teachers are judged on extremely limited criteria and ultimately judged to be succeeding or failing.

This approach is supported by the three major parties, with Labour starting the process under Tony Blair, David Blunkett and Lord Adonis.

The GERM can be seen as part of the neoliberal project that in conjunction with and through globalisation treats the world as a market and pursues unlimited growth based on over-consumption, plundering the planet's resources in the process and turning citizens, including young children, into consumers. Public monies, raised through taxation, are handed over to private companies for profit through privatisation and outsourcing.

A different vision

Faced with this fundamental challenge, the Green Party's education policy poses a very different vision for education:

Education should provide everyone with the knowledge and full range of skills they require to participate fully in society and lead a fulfilled life. The Green Party rejects market-driven models of education that see its role only in terms of international economic competitiveness and preparation for work.

Impact of the GERM on teachers and pupils

Before looking at our policy in detail, it is worth looking at what the pursuit of the GERM model has done to individuals in the education system, as well as the system itself.

In an adjournment debate, Caroline Lucas MP read into the record the testaments of teachers.[19] This is what one teacher said:

> We are in real danger of turning schools into exam factories … A number of times, I have had to cancel planned lessons in order to generate meaningless data to populate spreadsheets for senior members of staff. While assessment and feedback are a mandatory element of learning, I believe that the learning experience should be inspirational and innovative while promoting creativity, and yet constant streams of testing go against this.

Another explained:

> We need to see an end to this misguided notion that children are all the same and will progress in exactly the same way. Teaching them this early on in life that they are failures because they have not made what the government deems satisfactory progress is criminal and fosters feelings of inadequacy. We already know that how children feel about learning has a huge bearing on how much progress they make in the future.

Greens want to restore creativity to the classroom for the sake of both teachers and students, we want to raise the status of teachers and restore their professional autonomy, and we want both teachers and students to contribute to curriculum development.

The sword of Damocles hanging over schools – the enforcer, if you like, of the GERM and the accountancy method of assessing success via narrowly based data – is Ofsted. Schools have been dominated by WOW (what Ofsted wants) rather than their own assessment of

---

19   www.wembleymatters.blogspot.co.uk, accessed 12 December 2014. 'Caroline Lucas ensures powerful teacher voices are heard in Parliament.'

the needs of their children based on knowledge of them as human beings poised excitedly on the threshold of discovering all the wonders of the world. When schools are frightened of failure, of being labelled 'inadequate', with the public shame that goes along with that, they sometimes assume that any hint dropped by Ofsted on in-service courses or in the press is a 'requirement'. WOW replaces vision.

The second report of the Parliamentary Education Committee (March 2011)[20] heard evidence from Professor Nick Foskett of Keele University:

> Quite a number of people within ITE [initial teacher education] have experienced quite severe personal health issues as a result of their experiences of Ofsted inspection, particularly where those judgements were deemed to be unfair, unrealistic and based on inappropriate evidence and where there was a high-stakes negative consequence that came with that.

This was before a new stricter inspection framework was introduced and Michael Gove increased the politicisation of Ofsted's role by calling for schools deemed inadequate by Ofsted to be compulsorily converted into academies.

At the ATL conference in April 2014, teacher Simon Clarkson from Leicestershire spoke for many teachers when he said of Ofsted:

> I am a middle leader. I am told to ask for more and more from staff who are exhausted and have less and less to give. I see solid, dependable colleagues who I know are excellent teachers in tears … We need to stop the madness. We need to stop the Alice in Wonderland management of our schools and we need to fix the distorted looking glass that is Ofsted.[21]

---

20   www.publications.parliament.uk/pa/cm201011/cmselect/cmeduc/uc570-iii/uc57001. htm, accessed 9 January 2015.
21   https://news.tes.co.uk/b/news/2014/04/14/new-inspection-charter-needs-to-improve-standards-at-quot-broken-quot-ofsted-union-claims.aspx, accessed 9 January 2015.

An insightful child's comment on an Ofsted inspector was recorded by the Twitter account @TeacherROAR: 'My wise daughter on Ofsted inspection "He only wanted to know if I knew my target, not if I enjoyed the lesson or subject."'

We want to replace Ofsted with an independent National Council for Education Excellence (NCEE), working collaboratively with local authorities and schools and informed by educational research. Rather than seeking out failure and labelling schools, the NCEE will work with them. This alone is not enough because, in a sense, the current role of Ofsted is a consequence of the GERM – both its enforcer and its symptom. Our policy challenges all the features outlined by Sahlberg.

Fragmentation, competition, marketisation

As well as distorting the form of education taking place within institutions, the GERM, as implemented by the Conservative–Liberal Democrat coalition, has fragmented the educational system itself, to an extent where in some areas it can hardly be described as a system.

The academies programme, under both Labour and the coalition, has removed schools from local democratic accountability and, as Peter Newsam has argued, created a centrally funded 'nationalised' system that could be easily privatised. The introduction of academies has, as an integral part of the GERM project, set school against school in competition, and created a corporate rather than public service identity for education. Funding is based on pupil numbers and on the market presumption that failing schools will close. These premises undermine the cooperative ethos of the public sector.

At the same time, local democratic accountability is removed and governing bodies are less representative and often have little say because decision-making rests with the academy chain or sponsor. Michael Gove crusaded to get the reluctant primary sector to convert to academies. When this failed, he resorted to forced academisation. I experienced this at first hand when I supported parents campaigning against the forced academisation of Gladstone Park Primary School in Willesden, London.[22]

The school was downgraded from Grade 2 (good) to Grade 4 (inadequate) by Ofsted and immediately an 'academy broker', employed as a consultant by the Department for Education (DfE), was sent in to force its academisation – the unproven assumption being that academy status would magically improve performance. Parents and governors found themselves in correspondence with the disdainful head of a body with the joyous title of 'Brokerage and School Underperformance Division' of the DfE.

Parents did not recognise their school as described in the Ofsted report and pointed to aspects of the school that they valued which Ofsted did not comment on. They had a different vision of the purpose of education and what made a school 'good'. In correspondence with the DfE, the campaign found itself in Gove's version of Alice in Wonderland. One breathtaking example was the DfE's ruling that consultation about academisation would only take place *after* the decision had been made. The Green Party offered public support and contributed to the parent-led campaign at a strategic level.

To help them bring governing bodies into line, the DfE has the additional weapon of dissolving an uncooperative governing body and replacing it with an interim executive board, with carefully selected compliant members who oversee academisation.

The campaign at Gladstone Park had the support of some Labour councillors, but parents were frustrated by the failure of the Labour council itself to get behind the campaign and directly challenge the DfE. Eventually, the governing body won time to select their own preferred sponsor, although the DfE turned down their initial choice.

There is evidence that when a local authority gets strongly behind a campaign to prevent academisation, the battle can be won. In

---

22   www.savegladstoneparkschool.blogspot.com, accessed 12 December 2014.

Brighton, Green Party supporters and Caroline Lucas MP supported the campaign against the voluntary academisation of Hove Park School, while at the same time a local Conservative got together with a Labour Party member to write a joint pamphlet making the case for academies. As a result of community campaigning, the academisation proposal was shelved.

The Green Party opposes academies, supports campaigns against them, and is pledged to bring them back into the local authority family of schools. Similarly, we see free schools as another manifestation of the GERM. Originally marketed as a way of parents setting up their own schools, their purpose has become increasingly unclear. In some cases, fee-paying schools have applied to become free schools. Free schools have also contributed to fragmentation of the school system and have introduced a degree of confusion because they often open in areas where there is little or no demand. These schools sometimes fail to open on time and sometimes don't open at all or have very small numbers of children.

The government has interfered in the 'market' by ruling that any new school opening in a locality should be an academy or free school. In areas of school-place shortage, local authorities are not allowed to build new schools. This has resulted in the expansion of existing schools, often with playground space being eaten up by new classrooms. Some urban primary schools have expanded to five forms of entry, catering for more than 1,000 5–11-year-olds. This is far from our ideal of small, family-centred local schools accessible by foot. Ironically, free schools can then market themselves as just that.

Free schools, along with academies, represent a vehicle for eventually making all schools profit-making. They are outside local democratic accountability and make it almost impossible for local authorities to plan school places rationally. One of the selling points of the academisation and free school movement has been freedom from local authority 'control' and the freedoms they are said to enjoy regarding curriculum and the employment of staff. In fact, research has shown that there has only been limited use of these freedoms and, further, that many secondary schools converted only for the extra money involved.[23]

Green policy

One of the features of the current system is the introduction of formal teaching at an earlier and earlier age, in stark contrast to many other successful systems which have a later starting age for formal learning. Our system ignores all the research evidence on the importance of play as well as the stages of child development. Naturally lively and curious children are expected to sit still for long periods and inducted into 'schooling'.

We agree with the Too Much Too Soon campaign: 'There is no evidence to support such an early start and a great deal to suggest that it may be detrimental not only to [children's] well-being but also to their learning disposition and later academic achievement.'[24]

Our policy emphasises an early years focus on play, social education and confidence-building, with formal learning not starting until the age of six. We would abolish the nonsense of the phonics test.

The Green Party recognise that the national curriculum is too rigid and top-down, severely restricting teachers' ability to exercise creativity in their teaching in an exam-orientated 'sausage factory' system. We think schools and teachers should have more freedom to devise their own curriculum, and thus advocate a 'Learning Entitlement', which aims to set out broad goals of what children should experience, with teachers and students devising their own local content within that framework. This is linked to Article 12 of the UN Convention on the Rights of the Child, which states: 'Children's opinions on what and how they are taught should be taken into account.

---

23 http://news.tes.co.uk/b/news/2014/03/10/academies-shun-freedoms-available-to-them-survey-shows.aspxx, accessed 9 January 2015.

24 www.toomuchtoosoon.org, accessed 12 December 2014.

Children and young people's own interests and enthusiasms are the natural starting-point for productive learning, the roots from which a broad curriculum can grow.'

With Key Stage 1 and Key Stage 2 SATs abolished, children will no longer be 'taught to the test' with the stress and boredom that some experience, as well as the sense of failure felt by those who don't make the expected level.

The Learning Entitlement will include the development of essential numeracy and literacy skills and the core subjects but will also include speaking, thinking and listening skills; emotional literacy; academic and practical environmental education, including engagement with the outdoors; practical life skills; citizenship; and a language additional to English. Currently, the over-emphasis on academic achievement means that vocational, practical and creative subjects are undervalued. We would like to see school-leaving qualifications broadly based and would discourage too-early specialisation.

The Green Party is particularly concerned about the importance of good-quality sex and relationship education (SRE) and it is an issue that Caroline Lucas has taken up as an MP. This would be part of a child's Learning Entitlement.

We do not agree with the 'freedom' to employ unqualified teachers that is exercised to save money by some free schools and academies. We believe that all children should be taught by a qualified teacher or someone who is working towards qualification. The de-skilling of teachers has been going on for several decades through centrally dictated curricula and content, teaching to the test, and what often appears to be the imposition of particular teaching methods. Rather than educating children in the proper sense, teachers 'deliver' lessons and 'assess outcomes'. It is an industrial production-line model, with teachers as workers and children's scores as the product. Management are foremen, progress chasers and data accountants. Performance-related pay comes close to payment by results in this system and that is why we would abolish it.

In restoring the professional status of teachers we recognise the need for high-quality initial teacher education and subsequent in-service training and education. To make the most of those freedoms, through the independent National Council for Education Excellence and its links with educational research bodies, schools will have access to an evidence base for innovation rather than having to follow the latest ideas imposed by the Secretary of State.

These measures will give more freedom to teachers to exercise their professional judgement and will enable schools, within a broad entitlement framework, to devise a curriculum content for their particular local needs in partnership with children, parents and local community organisations.

As noted earlier, many schools are becoming huge institutions, which reinforce the industrial model and sometimes lead parents to prefer smaller free schools. At the same time, classes in local authority schools are much larger than those found in some private schools, often a reason for parents going private. We want, eventually, to reduce class sizes to twenty, and to keep schools to a maximum of 700 students.

Democratising education

Another Green Party core value is: 'We emphasise democratic participation and accountability by ensuring that decisions are taken at the closest practical level to those affected by them.'

We want to see a pupil school council and a parent forum or council in every school. In secondary schools and colleges, elected student council members will sit on school governing bodies and will have voting rights. Primary governing bodies will have a duty to regularly consult with their school councils.

We will seek to improve the democratic structure and accountability of local authorities and will support shared decision-making through a committee structure rather than a mayor or single-party cabinet system.

Our policy states:

> The Green Party recognises the key role of local authorities in the planning and provision of new school places, establishment of fair admissions policies, ensuring of equality of access for looked-after children and those with disabilities and special needs, and the provision of school support services. We will therefore strengthen local authorities through adequate funding and seek to enhance their local democratic accountability. We will review and reduce the powers of the Secretary of State.

The immediate problem is the funding cuts local authorities have experienced under the coalition's austerity regime. This has meant cutbacks in local authority school improvement teams and school support services. As a consequence, supporters of academisation and outsourcing have been able to argue that there is little benefit in remaining with the local authority school system if services have to be bought in anyway. The Green Party will actively work for the restoration, and eventual increase, of local authority funding.

Equality of access

We all know of the performance that some parents have to go through to get their children into their preferred choice of school, from church attendance by the non-religious to family relocation in order to be in a particular catchment area – with a resultant increase in house prices near particular schools. The latter becomes selection by wealth, which is of course also a feature of private schools qualification. Another less obvious form of selection is 'post-admissions selection', where children who don't 'fit in' are eased out of a secondary school in the early months of Year 7. The reason can be behaviour, or an expectation that they will bring down examination results. This can reflect racial or poverty issues and is a particular concern in academies.

The Green Party rejects selection by aptitude, ability or social class and aims for excellent all-ability schools with balanced intakes. We would remove charitable status from private schools with an eventual aim of absorbing them into the state system.

There is a potential conflict between the ideal of children being placed in local schools and the fact that there are often social and economic inequalities between areas. This could result in schools becoming segregated by race or class. Needs-based funding can help address this but we would see one of the roles of the local authority as ensuring a balanced intake as far as possible, particularly in comprehensive schools. Where catchment areas lead to de facto segregation, the local authority and schools should facilitate the mixing of children with other local schools.

The current emphasis on examination and test results – and a school's position in league tables – can lead to the exclusion from mainstream schooling of children with special educational needs. The Green Party supports the principle of inclusion so that all are entitled to be educated in a mainstream school, where their needs should be met in line with the UN Convention on the Rights of Persons with Disabilities.

At the same time, Green Party policy recognises that full integration may not be appropriate in all subjects in some exceptional cases – for example, where there are multiple learning difficulties. In the longer term, this should be addressed by having special resource units in mainstream schools. Every learner with disabilities will be entitled to an assessment of their needs that will identify equipment and facilities required, curriculum differentiation and learning styles, and any educational, professional and personal support that is needed.

Faith schools can contribute to inequality and a solution has to be achieved that balances the right of parents to choose the kind of education they prefer for their children with the need to challenge discrimination and religious intolerance. Greens would ensure that children are able to practise their faith in schools, for example through the provision of prayer or reflection space, but would abolish the requirement for a daily act of worship. If schools decided to continue an act of worship, alternative provision would have to be made for those deciding not to take part.

Religious instruction, as distinct from religious education, would only take place out of school curriculum times. Privately funded schools run by religious organisations would have to reflect the inclusive nature of British society and become part of the local authority admissions system.

Higher education and beyond

Today's students have been let down by Labour and the coalition, who have trebled tuition fees. Currently standing at £9,000 per year, they burden graduates with a degree and a £45,000 debt.

Our higher education is now the most expensive for students in Europe. And yet it is a broken system, and costs more than that which it replaced. The benefit has gone to the universities and their higher echelons, where staff have had massive pay rises while undergraduate courses suffer. Universities are now practically in the private sector.

Greens believe that education should be free to all as part of the common good, so we will end tuition fees and support student living costs with our proposed basic income. We want to bring universities into the real world so will connect them with local schools through the Widening Participation Programme. We will support mature students and their families in recognition of the fact that education is not just a linear process through primary, secondary, further and higher education but something that should enrich, challenge and stimulate people throughout life.

Instead of an education system based on unsustainable economic growth, competition and acquisition, education for the common good will be life-enhancing for the individual and will aim to build a more equal and inclusive society.

Martin Francis is Brent Green Party spokesperson on Children and Families. He is a school governor and former head-teacher. Martin runs outdoor education days for primary school pupils. @WembleyMatters

Chapter 5

Women's Politics

SARAH COPE

Growth of feminism

A few years ago, it wasn't uncommon for women, particularly younger women, to begin a sentence with the words 'I'm not a feminist, but...' They would then usually go on to highlight one of the many sexist injustices in our society, which might range from street harassment to unequal pay.

A few years on and everyone is a feminist. OK, maybe not Nigel Farage! But being a feminist has become a badge of honour. 'Feminism: the radical idea that women are equal to men' as placards sometimes proclaim on equality marches. Or, as writer Maya Angelou succinctly put it, 'I am a feminist. I've been female for a long time now. I'd be stupid not to be on my own side.'

This surge in feminism has come at an opportune time, when old-fashioned sexism seems to be on the rise. From 'slut-shaming' to the seemingly never-ending public assault on women's bodies (the normalisation of plastic surgery, fat-shaming, extortionate anti-ageing products), the promise of the end of sexism, a time of equality when outdated male attitudes towards women were a thing of the past, has proved hollow.

This fourth wave of feminism, supported by young women and

veteran women's activists alike – together with men who have also found that gender strictures, compelling them to be strong, silent and dismissive of women, just haven't worked for them – is promising to sweep away the old order and bring in a new, enlightened age, where women will be given equal pay for equal work and no longer have to walk around in a state of paralysing self-doubt, fixated on their perceived 'flaws'. Writers such as Caitlin Moran, with her funny and accessible book *How To Be a Woman*, have helped popularise feminism even further.

Indeed, such is the strength of this feminist surge – which has come at the same time as a growing disillusionment with mainstream 'business as usual' politics – that there have recently been calls for a new 'feminist political party' to be set up.

It's not surprising that such calls have been made when in today's House of Commons men outnumber women four to one. It's worth remembering that there are more millionaires around the current Cabinet table than there are women. Indeed, in the words of the Fawcett Society, it is clear that if you're not at the table, you're on the menu. In other words, if women are not there to represent women, issues that affect us most get swept aside.

Fawcett have predicted that the number of female MPs will actually fall after this general election. The UK is, at the time of writing, sixty-fifth in the world in terms of the number of women in Parliament, behind countries such as Rwanda, Mozambique and Uganda. The thought of us slipping even further down this list, particularly at a time of such a growth in feminism, seems unthinkable. The effects of not having enough women MPs during the disastrous reign of the coalition government are plain to see.

Women have been hit the hardest by austerity measures; benefit cuts and public sector cuts hurt women the most, and with women making up the majority of the ever-increasing number of low-paid workers, this 'triple whammy' has disadvantaged the most vulnerable. The statistics speak for themselves: to date, 74 per cent of

£22 billion of austerity 'savings' have come from women's pockets. In short, a huge proportion of women are paying for the mistakes made by the privileged, out-of-touch few who see fit to play our financial markets as if they're a casino.

At the same time as these swingeing cuts, additional cuts to legal aid, domestic abuse services, and carers' and childcare support have exacerbated an already calamitous situation. It only takes one or two things – a relationship crisis, a children's centre closing, a mental health issue – and a woman and indeed her children's lives can be sent into a downward spiral.

With so much to cope with, no wonder young women are one of the groups least likely to vote. This is played out on the doorstep; when canvassing for the Green Party, I have lost count of the number of young women saying politics is of no interest to them. And yet they will then go on to talk passionately about schools, about access to health provision, about the environment. That, I tell them, is politics.

We need more of these women to become activists – which many of them indeed are doing, as grassroots campaign groups harness the power of social media, campaigning on local and national issues as multifarious as the installation of new pedestrian crossings outside schools and the removal of naked women from the pages of a national newspaper.

We also need more women in the corridors of power and I would agree with those commentators previously mentioned who believe that a feminist political party is sorely needed, right here, right now.

And I have good news for all those who dream of that political party: it already exists. It's called the Green Party.

Need to be convinced? Take a look at just a few of our women-centric policies that certainly show we are a party which strives at all times to be truly feminist. Our leader doesn't need to wear a T-shirt that proclaims 'This Is What A Feminist Looks Like', because this is what a feminist political party looks like.

Our policies are researched, drafted and voted for by our members, not think tanks responding to what focus groups have told them will be vote-winners. They are the policies that protect, not ignore, the vulnerable and marginalised many. This is, as deputy leader Shahrar Ali has put it, 'the politics of imagination'. And goodness knows we need that sort of politics right now.

Promoting women in politics

We live in interesting times, where the winds of change constantly threaten to blow through that impressive if stuffy edifice the Houses of Parliament, leaving it unrecognisable. Anyone who has traversed those endless corridors, that maze of wood panelling, which resembles nothing so much as a private all-boys' school (funny, that!), will no doubt agree that change is necessary.

First of all, we need more diverse people representing us as MPs. I recently spoke at an event where Labour MP Diane Abbott was also present. She said that she agreed with a Tory friend of hers who had opined that you need 'f***-off money' in order to be an MP. I was shocked by this comment. The implication was that, unless you had lots of money, Abbott explained, you would be liable to be 'bought off' by groups who had certain interests and wanted you to work on their behalf in Parliament.

There is much wrong with this idea. First of all, would you not hope that an MP would have enough integrity that they would not even consider being 'bought off'? Furthermore, in making this statement, Abbott seems to swallow wholesale the idea that politics is for the privileged few, and that this is not a problem.

But it is a huge problem, for reasons already touched upon. How to change things? One way in which the whole make-up of Westminster could be altered – and made to be actually representative of the people it is supposed to serve – is to allow 'job-share' MPs. This has been a Green Party policy for several years, and we are in the process of trying to make it a reality. At the time of writing, we are working with a high-profile legal team to launch a judicial review into the possibility of job-share MPs, using the Equality Act as our weapon of choice.

Imagine the difference job-sharing would make to those who, previously, due to caring responsibilities, lack of time or money, disability or a myriad of other hurdles, would never even have considered that being an MP was for them. Suddenly, the corridors of power would be full of new ideas, new energy, and those who are marginalised and often sidelined by traditional politics would at last have a say and be properly represented. What better way to reinvigorate politics and enliven peoples' interest in voting?

Steps have, of course, been taken to change the make-up of our political class, perhaps most notably with Labour's 'all-women' shortlists, introduced for the 1997 election. This move was much maligned, with critics claiming that women should be selected 'on merit'; Ann Widdecome even claimed that the suffragettes would have thrown themselves under the King's horse to protest about 'positive discrimination'.

Hardly! When the scales are tipped so far in the favour of white men, surely rebalancing them slightly with all-women shortlists in some constituencies is only common sense? Also, those who criticise this measure tend to think that women selected thus have 'an easy ride'. Could you be any more patronising to women?! Labour MP Gisela Stuart, herself selected via an all-women shortlist, has said that right at the beginning of the contest she and the other women nominees got together and agreed they would fight tooth and nail for the candidacy. And let's not forget: detractors would be looking for any opportunity to point out the failings, the perceived weaknesses, of a woman selected thus, and she would have to be ten times better than any man (as well as being subject to crass newspaper articles about her appearance, as we recently saw after a Cabinet reshuffle; 'the Downing Street catwalk', indeed!).

But how are we doing in terms of promoting women within our

ranks – of practising what we preach, in other words? In the 2010 general election, the Green Party managed to field 32 per cent female candidates, but this was only after a very last-minute push to get that percentage up. This was the highest percentage of female candidates that any party managed to field, though that isn't saying very much. Ninety-two per cent of selections had only one nominee, and 67 per cent had only male nominees. Clearly there was room for improvement.

A group of us within the party (inventively titled 'Green Party Women') got together and worked on a plan to get more women candidates selected this time around. At the party's autumn conference in 2012, we passed a motion agreeing to aim for *at least* 50 per cent women candidates in general elections and PR elections such as the European elections.

On top of that, in spring 2013, the party passed a motion stating that for each general election constituency candidate selection, if no woman comes forward by close of nominations, the process would have to be re-opened for an additional period to offer another opportunity.

Baby steps, perhaps, but ones that send out a clear message to all our local parties across England and Wales: you need to be promoting, supporting and training up women in your local parties. For it would be no good if we were a party of strong feminist principles, yet failed to address issues within our own ranks where women were being under-represented and sidelined. It does happen sometimes; perfect humans we are not. But at least we address the problem and try to solve it, rather than deny its existence outright.

What, though, of those aforesaid policies which mark us out as a feminist party? There are many policies I could mention, but due to space constraints I will only mention a select few here. For more information, please do take a look at our Green Party Women website www.greenpartywomen.org.uk, or at our dedicated policy site www.policy.greenparty.org.uk.

Childcare and maternity

Caring responsibilities fall to women the vast majority of the time. I write this after four hours' sleep (due to the fact that my three-year-old likes to sit on my head for most of the night), so I speak from experience about how caring responsibilities can impact upon one's ability to contribute to society!

Childcare provision in this country is reportedly the most expensive in Europe, and yet childcare is seen, unjustly, as a lowly profession, despite the fact that those engaged in bringing up the next generation are shaping the world of tomorrow in the most profound way imaginable. What could be more important than how our children turn out, particularly as they will inherit a world of problems – climate change, economic instability – which will need great ingenuity to set right?

The Green Party, then, has a childcare policy which addresses the gaps in services and the need for childcare to be elevated as a profession. We also would set up more community childcare, where people are encouraged to pool resources, reducing isolation and making sure we reach out to those most in need of services (something the previous Labour government's SureStart Centres were accused of failing to do).

And if we take one step back, before childcare issues impact upon a woman's life, we come to the problematic issue of maternity services. Nowhere, surely, is the impoverished nature of our beloved NHS more heartbreakingly apparent than when one is pregnant and trying to get decent ante- and post-natal care. A shortage of midwives, an increasing demand that women accept medical intervention, a lack of support – or a serious inability to provide provision – for home births for those who want them, and we can see why it was reported that an estimated ten million women in the UK are suffering from post-birth trauma at any one time.

The Green Party's maternity policy is nothing especially radical: it is common sense. We would prioritise continuity of care, so that women are able to see the same midwife throughout their pregnancy and birth. We would ensure that all birthing options are available to women – no coercion, no 'postcode lotteries', just equal access and decent services.

All of this is the least women deserve at this most challenging of times in their lives. You may wonder how we would pay for all this, but when you consider, for example, that litigation following hospital errors during birth accounted for £3.1 billion during the years 2000–10 – and let's not forget the human cost – it is easy to see why providing decent maternity services makes sense on every level.

Post-natally, we would ensure that women who want to breastfeed are given the support they need, including introducing a law with significant fines for companies whose employees attempt to stop women breastfeeding on their premises (as has been successfully implemented in Scotland). This does still happen to women, believe it or not: shamed for performing the most natural of acts in public. It seems that it's vile to breastfeed in public, but perfectly OK for a national newspaper to print pictures of naked breasts on a daily basis.

We would also introduce shared maternity and paternity leave for the first month after birth or adoption, then provide for a total of twenty-two months, which may be shared so that the parent taking less leave takes a minimum of six months, except for single parents. This leave would be paid up to 90 per cent of salary up to a reasonable level.

Not every woman who becomes pregnant will of course avail herself of maternity services; for those who become pregnant and do not want to be, it is vital we have reliable abortion services. Over recent years, several attempts to curtail abortion access have been attempted, most notably by Tory MP Nadine Dorries, who, mystifyingly, seems to have made punishing those in desperate need of abortion services her own personal crusade.

As many of us can testify, there is a world of difference between being pregnant when you want to be (which can be gruelling enough!)

and being pregnant when it is the last thing on earth that you want to be. Our current abortion services are very antiquated, with the need to acquire two doctors' signatures before the procedure can be carried out. The Green Party would remove that requirement, and would also ensure that midwives and nurses who are appropriately qualified can perform abortions, as well as removing other restrictions that are medically unnecessary, with the aim of improving access to NHS abortions.

At the same time, we would improve sex education, so that abortion rates would hopefully be lowered and also that young people of all genders would be confident and assertive as they begin to navigate the complex area of sex and relationships. Sex education under the Green Party would not just be about putting condoms on bananas (as fun as that might be), but would also focus on the difficult business of emotions and relationships.

Crisis centres

The austerity cuts have hit women hard, and one of the ways in which they have impacted on women is the slashing of funding for services the most vulnerable women rely on, such as refuges and rape crisis centres. One woman is killed in the UK every three days by a current or former partner and, as Women's Aid has pointed out, 'a wrong decision in this field can cost lives'. There was already an issue of limited funding for these critical services, with applications for funding taking up valuable time, but now with resources even scarcer, things look yet bleaker, with Women's Aid reporting that 60 per cent of refuge services have had council funding removed, resulting in widespread job losses within the sector.

The Green Party would implement its model policy for dealing with domestic abuse (including domestic violence) which recognises that the needs and desires of the victims must be paramount, and that all service providers who come into contact with potentially vulnerable women need to be trained to provide appropriate assistance.

Furthermore, we would ensure that rape crisis centres and domestic violence centres receive guaranteed funding from core budgets so that they are not forced to operate in a state of constant funding uncertainty.

Women seeking asylum

A group of women who are vulnerable many times over are women seeking asylum in the UK. The Green Party has been working with the campaign group Women for Refugee Women, who are demanding that women no longer be held in detention centres. A report the group released in early 2014 revealed that a shocking one in five of the women in Yarl's Wood Immigration Removal Centre had tried to kill themselves, so desperate had they been about being essentially imprisoned for no crime whatever, and at the thought of facing deportation to a country where their life would most probably be at grave risk.

The Green Party recently augmented its already refreshingly humane policy on asylum seekers – which recognises the potential risks to, and needs of, women seeking asylum, including issues of forced marriage, female genital mutilation and domestic violence – by adding a commitment to close down detention centres, full stop. They are inhumane, expensive and counterproductive, meaning that asylum seekers are more likely to go underground in a bid to escape being detained. They are particularly difficult for women asylum seekers, a disproportionate amount of whom will have survived rape and other forms of abuse in their home countries, and may now have to endure being watched over by a male guard while in detention. Indeed, with allegations of sexual harassment by male guards at Yarl's Wood, there is even more reason for these 'prisons for the innocent' to be closed down.

Decriminalising sex work

Another group of women in our society who are particularly vulnerable, largely due to the inadequacies of the current law, are sex workers. As long as it remains illegal for more than one woman to work out of a premises, sex workers – male and female, let's not forget – will remain vulnerable and at risk of violence. Indeed, as with asylum seekers, the current way we have of dealing with this – of persecuting the vulnerable and thus driving them further underground – means that their vulnerability is exacerbated. This particularly applies, in the case of sex workers, to trafficked women.

We owe it to the 80,000 people who work in prostitution in the UK, most of whom are in poverty and 70 per cent of whom are single mothers, to make their work safer. The Green Party would therefore decriminalise sex work, meaning that workers in the sex industry would enjoy the same rights as other workers, such as the right to join unions, as well as the right to choose whether to work cooperatively with others. Decriminalisation would also help facilitate the collection of taxes due from those involved in sex work. Legal discrimination against sex workers would be ended (for example, in child custody cases, where evidence of sex work is often taken to mean that a person is an unfit parent).

The Green Party recognises that, although people should be free to engage in sex work if they wish, this is an industry which can be more exploitative than others, and those who work in it should be adequately protected against such exploitation. There should be zero tolerance of coercion, violence and sexual abuse (including child abuse).

Regular health checks should be available to all sex workers, free of charge, to protect both them and their clients.

Some sex workers choose to work from home, or in residential premises, like some other trades. Such use of primarily residential premises would be permitted without a licence being required, subject to the avoidance of nuisance and abuse. This exemption from licensing requirements should still apply if more than one person works in such premises, provided that such activities take place on a sufficiently small scale that they are not tantamount to a commercial brothel.

The Green Party's policy on sex work remains contentious, and we shouldn't pretend that this isn't an area that divides opinion, even within the party itself. However, basing our policy, as we always endeavour to, on current evidence and research, the above remains the most sensible route to take on an issue that will never go away.

Countries such as Sweden who have criminalised the buying of sex, but (bizarrely) decriminalised the selling of sex, have found that numbers of sex workers have not decreased, and that attacks on women have actually increased. One reason for this is that street-based sex workers have to work in more remote locations, and have less time to assess the safety of the situation before getting into a client's car, so anxious are the latter to avoid being arrested for buying sex. This is clearly no solution, unlike full decriminalisation, which seems to many of us the 'least worst' option.

This is clearly a difficult area to discuss without coming across as the 'middle-class rescuer', though it is important to note that the Green Party's policy has had much input from sex workers past and present, and as such is grounded in lived experience.

There are many more policies I would love to describe at length; I haven't even touched upon, for example, measures we would take in the workplace, such as introducing a law to ensure that boards of major companies are at least 40 per cent female (following the model in Norway); insisting that all large and medium-sized companies carry out equal pay audits, and that they then redress any inequalities that are uncovered; and that the law be changed to make joint suits for equal pay cases simpler.

Already our one Green MP, Caroline Lucas, together with Green Party councillors up and down the country, as well as passionate party activists, are working to put these well-thought-out policies into practice. Just imagine what additional MPs in the House of Commons could achieve should you vote Green this May.

A vote for the Greens is a feminist vote; a claim that, looking at our track record and policies, it is not clear that any other political party can make.

Sarah Cope has been an active member of the Green Party for over a decade and is chair of Green Party Women. She used to be a radio producer and is now a freelance journalist. @GreenSarahCope

Chapter 6

Welfare

NOEL LYNCH

This is a personal romp through Green Party policies on social welfare rather than a full exposition of the issues, which would require many more pages. Our detailed policies can be found at www.policy.greenparty.org.uk.

We live in unsettling times. Many of the securities that our parents and grandparents fought for – a functioning National Health Service, free education and an affordable home – now look out of reach for most of us. Coupled with this, climate change is bringing unpredictable and threatening weather patterns.

People feel let down by politicians, and there has been an explosion in political activism. People want to do things differently and aren't afraid to be bold and challenging.

The Green Party is benefiting from a 'Green surge' – our membership doubled in 2014 and is still rising. As membership officer of the London Green Party I have seen this at first hand. We normally had about three new members per day – now we are getting on average thirty per day! This is at a time when the prevailing expert opinion is saying that people do not join political parties. At our new member events, I ask, 'Why did you join the Green Party?' Common replies are: 'I finally decided that I had to do something and I saw that the Green Party is the only one prepared to take a stand', 'I feel let down

by Labour', 'I was a Lib Dem supporter and voted for them to keep
the Tories out. Instead, they put them in', 'I got tired of voting tac-
tically', 'I got tired of shouting at the TV'.

People are fed up with policies that tinker around the edges. They
want real change that benefits people and the environment. A real
change from austerity and welfare cuts to investment in decent
jobs. A real change from privatisation benefiting 1 per cent of the
population to public management of essential services not driven
by corporate greed. A real change from subsidies for fracking and
dependence on fossil fuels to a sustainable world we can pass on
to our children and grandchildren. These are the reasons for the
Green surge.

While environmental concerns brought me to the Green Party – in
particular the Chernobyl disaster and the realisation that environmental problems needed to be tackled at local and international levels
– it was the social policies of the Green Party that really inspired. Of
these, the citizen's income could usher in real change at a grassroots
level. In so far as it is possible to remedy social problems purely by
financial means, the implementation of this policy will enable people to have a more flexible approach to work, retirement and caring
for others.

A citizen's income is an unconditional and non-withdrawable
income payable to each individual as a right of citizenship. It will
not be subject to means testing and there will be no requirement to
be either working or seeking work. Everyone in a civilised society is
entitled to have their basic needs met so there should be no strings
to the allowance that guarantees provision.

Think of the changes this could usher in: people would be able
to work on their hobbies, small grassroots businesses could bloom,
grandparents would be able to look after their grandchildren, writers and artists would thrive. We would have a population of people
happy at their work, which would enhance the health of the nation.

On earnings over and above the guaranteed citizen's income, rates of income tax would be set according to the principle that those on higher incomes will pay higher marginal rates of tax.

Health

Greens oppose moves toward an American-style privatised system and PFIs which are holding the NHS to ransom.

Health is the condition in which individuals and communities achieve their full physical, intellectual, social and spiritual potential. Health for individuals is only possible in the context of a healthy environment and society. The healthy society is one which guarantees a safe and clean environment; material security for all its citizens; good work; adequate housing; a balanced and unpolluted diet and clean water; appropriate education; a safe transport system; accessible and sensitive public services; equality of opportunity; and a secure present and hope for the future. All Green Party policies are designed to promote the health of individuals, communities and society.

The citizen's income policy would simplify a lot of the complications of the benefits system which is itself a cause of stress, ill health and suicide; and the Green Party plans for home insulation and renewable energy would give people the comfort and warmth they need in their homes. We will not force vulnerable people to choose between eating and heating.

The organisation and use of health care services is only one of the factors which impacts on our health. To a large extent, factors such as where we live, the state of our environment, genetics, our income and education level, and our relationships with friends and family all have considerable impacts on health. However, a willingness and ability to care for its vulnerable members are essential features of a compassionate society. Free market mechanisms cannot adequately meet health needs or effectively constrain costs. Proper healthcare for all and the responsible use of resources both require the continued provision of well-financed and publicly funded health services.

Healthcare is not a commodity to be bought or sold. The National Health Service must provide healthcare, free at the point of need, funded through taxation. It must be a public service funded, run by and accountable to local and national government and free from all privatisation, whether administration, healthcare provision, support services or capital ownership. The NHS is concerned with healthcare provision and should not be subject to market forces either internal or external.

Greens would develop health services which place as much emphasis on illness prevention, health promotion and the development of individual and community self-reliance as on the treatment and cure of disease. All services will be available without charge at the time of need.

The Green Party knows that we are all interdependent and that many people need support at some stage in their lives. The basic aim is that all people should be able to lead an empowered and fulfilled life. We believe that every individual in society has an equal right to food, water, warmth and housing.

Grandparents

As a grandparent myself and founder of Green Seniors, I have a particular interest in the subject which is often ignored. Grandparents are often the only reason that their children can go out to work. They shoulder many responsibilities and traumas. Apart from the child, grandparents and great-grandparents are usually the innocent parties. It broke my mother's heart when she was barred all access to her only great-grandchild on the breakup of her grandson's marriage. The present government promised to rectify this and give grandparents rights of access, but did not.

The Greens would legislate to give working grandparents the same right to request flexi-work as parents if caring for grandchildren.

Disabled people

The Green Party has endorsed the social model of disability where there is a recognition that society has put up barriers which prevents disabled people with different impairments from becoming and being full and active citizens. The Green Party is strongly committed to valuing, empowering and supporting people with illness and disabilities.

Equal opportunities must start from day one and to this end the Green Party supports the purpose of the Disability Discrimination Act (DDA), which is to ensure disabled people have the same opportunities as non-disabled people to participate in civic life. We recognise that all disabled people, including people with sensory, learning, physical and mental health impairments, should be able to live in the community with appropriate support if desired.

Social services tend to be institutionalised and inflexible and based on non-disabled people's perceptions of what disabled people need. This has prevented disabled people from determining their own lives.

It is important for people with disabilities to be part of the socialisation process that their able-bodied peers experience. Children with disabilities should be given support to do activities independently of their parents. They need support and opportunities for personal development. Personal care and support for disabled people should be provided free, so that they can operate from a financial foundation equal to their peers. This includes any expenses incurred from having a disability, such as communication aids, interpretation and accommodation adaptations, mental health support, personal mobility aids, learning support, counselling, psychotherapy, art and music therapy or other therapies as appropriate.

We would always seek to ensure emphasis is placed on enabling and empowering people to make choices about their lives. Skills training for jobs or independent living will be provided. Some disabled people need support to manage their own care packages. Each local authority will fund independent living services (Centres for Inclusive Living) to provide advice, advocacy and support to help people manage their care packages. We recognise that much social welfare work is done by volunteers, charities, helplines and family members, including children. Such individuals would be helped by citizen's income and proper, stable funding of voluntary organisations.

We support the current position of benefits; however we would work towards streamlining it in the short and medium term and replacing it with citizen's income in the long term.

We recognise that where social welfare support is provided year-round by family members or friends exclusively, there may arise a need for respite from the duties this involves. Such breaks are vital in that they ensure carers get the time we all need to rest from work. We also recognise that breaks from caring work enable carers to go on caring. Many respite and day care centres have been closed in recent years, and the buildings sold to the private sector, in order that financial savings be realised by health and social services departments. We will support existing respite centres and fund the replacement of respite care centres where they are needed. The short-term capital investment will be offset in the long term by fewer family breakdowns and fewer admissions to permanent institutions.

Workers and trade unions

Greens have an absolute commitment to supporting trade unions and the right to strike. We would repeal the anti-union legislation introduced by Margaret Thatcher and continued by Labour. Empowering people is a key element in the development of a Green society and economy. The Green Party is committed to workplace democracy, whereby undertakings shall be managed cooperatively through the involvement of those who work in them and the communities they serve.

Enshrining rights in law gives people a means of protection from injustice. Workers' rights offer protection against exploitation under our existing economic system. Our long-term aim is to end the oppressive and exploitative nature of economic relations and develop a society of equality and economic justice. In such a society, rights would still need to be guaranteed in law, but there would be much less recourse to the law in order to protect those rights.

Individual workers need appropriate protection under the law. This means: 1) a set of basic rights for all employees; 2) a package of measures to support the self-employed and small businesses; 3) a charter for volunteers and carers.

Workplace democracy will help us to attain these long-term aims. However, it must go hand in hand with other reforms that deal with discrimination, the power of the state, the ownership of land and the control of information. All these influence our ability to control our working lives, which in turn affects an individual's ability to care for the planet.

For rights to be upheld and defended, access to relevant information and means of enforcement must be ensured. Every worker must have the right, from the outset of their employment, to access effective remedies to enforce their rights, including adequate rights for workers' representatives to inspect and obtain information.

Recognising that income inequality underlies and fuels most of the social problems confronting us in Britain today, we propose that in all undertakings, the maximum wage paid to any member of staff should not exceed ten times that paid (pro rata) to the lowest-paid worker. In addition, no member of staff in an organisation should receive an annual bonus exceeding the annual wage of the lowest-paid worker in that organisation.

We will support moves towards global labour standards and a global living wage, in close collaboration with trade unions, citizens groups, employers and the International Labour Organization and with as full as possible consultation of workers and citizens themselves, to ensure that such steps bring about genuine improvements in the lives and incomes of low-paid workers. Benefits will be paid equally to all people over sixteen years of age, with additional payments to pensioners and people with disabilities or special needs.

The Green Party supports the right of working people to form and join free democratic and self-governing trade unions, without restriction by employer or government. Greens share the unions' belief in working together to give individuals more say in their own lives. We recognise the achievements of trade unions in protecting and improving their members' terms and conditions of employment. We note that such benefits have accrued not only to union members but also to their fellow workers. Health and safety at work is a particular example. Unions have also acted to improve the social welfare of the wider community, and have a wider political role.

We are determined that the United Kingdom shall move to a green society and economy. The fundamental changes that process brings will be reflected in changing forms and roles for trade unions. Unions already play a part in wider issues affecting their members. The Green Party is committed to supporting and encouraging this process of change in unions. In particular, we envisage a major role for unions in promoting workplace democracy. We also believe that reformed trades councils could have a valuable role in their local communities.

We support the right to join a trade union, and condemn discrimination by employers against union members. We will enact a statutory right to join a union, which will apply to all workers of any occupation or profession; this will include members of the police, security and armed services. We support unions taking the unwaged and unemployed into membership. Discrimination against union members, and, in particular, refusal of employment or dismissal on grounds of union membership, shall be illegal.

Workers engaged in industrial action would retain their right to employment and would be protected from unfair dismissal on account of that action. They shall have the rights to strike and to picket peacefully; the latter will include rights to use the public highway for picketing and to speak with anyone crossing the picket line.

A code of practice shall cover the use of these rights; it will emphasise non-violent picketing and non-provocative policing of pickets. Dismissal of a worker for refusing to cross a picket line is unfair. Lockouts shall be illegal.

Payments to workers under our proposed citizen's income scheme will not depend upon their being in work, and thus will be made to strikers. Prior to the introduction of that scheme, we believe that workers on strike and their families should receive full social security benefits.

We will require medium- and large-sized companies to be accountable to their employees and to the general public by including on their management boards employee-elected directors and independent directors to represent the interests of consumers.

The creation of a floor of individual rights at work, the ending of discrimination and the introduction of the citizen's income scheme will help transform the contract of employment into more of a partnership than an exchange between an 'employer' and 'employee'.

Advice services

Having worked for six years as a volunteer advisor at the East Finchley Advice Centre, I saw at first hand the absolute need for free advice.

Barnet Council took a very short-term attitude to our services. While we had a small grant, the council took much of it back in rent! We saved the council thousands of pounds in staff hours. Much of the work consisted in filling in forms for our clients and explaining their entitlements. We hear a lot about 'benefit cheats' and 'dole scroungers' but we saw little evidence of that. What we did see was a complete lack of help from the government or council in explaining people's entitlements. I estimate that there is much more money lost in the underpaying of benefits than in benefit cheating. And as for the real tax-dodgers – the rich and big business – well, the government seems to have neither the ability nor the interest in tackling the issue.

The Green Party would fund and support local advice centres, free legal aid and money advice services. Legal aid would also be provided for cases brought before the labour courts. The attack on the welfare benefits and services is an attack on the welfare of us all.

The benefit cap will mean that tens of thousands of families will have to move out of London and the south-east in particular, uprooting children from schools and wrecking relationships. Families will be forced to move to cheaper accommodation where jobs are harder to find. This will do nothing to reduce the cost of unemployment.

We in the Green Party believe that rather than cutting benefits to the poorest and most vulnerable we should increase taxes on the richer sectors of society and make sure that they pay their fair share. This would protect benefits and also pay for a programme of 'green jobs' which would create employment and transform our energy production, transportation and housing. Our Green New Deal would create 1 million 'green' jobs, insulate thousands of homes and help combat climate change.

I read recently that billionaires pay less than 1 per cent tax. The real truth is that there is plenty of money around. It's just in the wrong hands in an unfair economy!

Noel Lynch is a long-time Green activist and former member of the London Assembly. He runs a green charity shop – The Green Room – in Islington. @noellynchlondon

Chapter 7

Home Affairs

PETER CRANIE

Green politics requires us to think in the long term and not just about electability in the short term, so our domestic policies will never be set to fit the agenda of those individuals who own the media in Britain. We will instead look at what is needed for a healthier and happier society, making our case for a better future.

Race relations and migration

Over the last few years, the issue that has persistently ranked as the highest concern for people in Britain has been race relations/immigration.[25] The obvious question to ask is: why are these two issues lumped together?

We've seen UKIP exploit a perception that we've had enough immigrants come into the UK and that it is time to close the borders. UKIP's remedy is to leave the EU, regain full national border control and impose an Australian-style points system to those who wish to move to the UK.

The national focus on immigration has been emotive and dominated by how people feel about it. There has been little discussion

25   *The Economist*/Ipsos MORI September 2014 Issues Index.

of migration globally and the reasons people are pushed out of their homes; and the economic argument has been reduced to a 'snapshot' approach instead of a rational discussion about the needs of our society in the coming decades.

The five biggest nationality groupings arriving in the UK in 2013 were from China, India, Poland, Australia and the US. Chinese immigration is up, with the increase due to Chinese students coming to study at UK universities. We know that international students pay substantially more than UK students for their fees. A 2013 report by HSBC calculated that the average international student fee at a UK university was $19,291.[26]

Universities in the UK already feel that the anti-immigration rhetoric from this government has led to a 51 per cent drop in postgraduate enrolments from India and Pakistan.[27] The removal of this stream of income from universities has an immediate impact in terms of the education available to the UK-based student, but in the longer term it also means that talented graduates from India, Pakistan and the like will be looking elsewhere for their future career.

Unsurprisingly, there is very little discussion of Americans or Australians (and excuse the phrasing) 'coming over here and taking our jobs'. Immigrants from these countries are perceived to be white and English speaking. The immigration that UKIP wants people to focus on is from Eastern Europe and elsewhere. The narrative in the media is that Britain is being 'flooded' or 'swamped' by unskilled workers but that doesn't reflect the reality about immigration in Britain today.

The exaggerated fears of immigration, benefit fraud and crime will be played out in this election campaign but the Green Party will meet fear with the facts. The bigger issue for us is the huge disparity of wealth in the UK. The wealth of households and not-for-profit

---

26 'Australia most expensive country for international study, but the tide may turn', 13 August 2014, www.about.hsbc.com.au/news-and-media, accessed 12 December 2014.

27 'University chief Sir Christopher Snowden claims government immigration policy puts off foreign students', *The Independent*, 9 September 2014.

organisations in the UK is £8.5 trillion.[28] Shared equally, that would be around £135,000 for every child, woman and man in Britain. In an equal Britain, an average family of four would have assets of over £500,000.

We've made huge advances in equality legislation, but women are still not paid the same as men and unemployment is higher in many minority ethnic groups. Disabled and LGBTIQ individuals continue to face indirect and direct discrimination, not least when a representative of one of the ruling parties feels it is still acceptable to suggest those with disabilities can get paid less than the minimum wage. Instead, we need a vision of Britain where the minimum wage is at least £10 per hour and provides an adequate living for those who earn it. We need a country where the gap between rich and poor narrows considerably and consistently over decades.

Drugs policy

For many, crime is a daily problem in their community, from anti-social behaviour to reckless speeding that endangers the lives of every road user. Fear of crime is an even bigger issue. It may inhibit some individuals from living the full and free life they want.

When research points to the causal factors of crime as community deprivation and income inequalities resulting from unemployment, and that it is concentrated and associated with factors such as homelessness, poor health, parenting issues, drugs and alcohol misuse, school exclusion, leaving care and prison,[29] then we know what we have to do. A more equal society will have lower crime rates and the political approach to crime must be to tackle these problems.

A Green approach would be to look at those groups who are most affected by crime and at real, evidence-based approaches

---

28   'Headline numbers: How much is everything in the UK worth?', BBC Online.
29   Social Policy Research Unit (SPRU), 'The drivers of social exclusion: a review of the literature – summary' (ODPM Social Exclusion Unit, 2004).

to tackle the causes. Those groups affected disproportionately by hate crimes, whether it relates to social disadvantage, disability, sexuality or race, can look at our approach to these issues in this election. We want solutions that work, but these are not sound bites or slogans.

It's often the individual cases that provoke outrage against minority groups or the socially excluded that will come up in an election campaign. The perceptions of focus groups in a few dozen marginal constituencies matter far more in our dysfunctional political system than a practical approach that would really address the problems. What we need is real investment in solutions that work and a willingness to take on the controversial issues.

The war on drugs has failed. This is the view of the overwhelming majority of British people.[30] So the continued macho posturing of politicians to show who can be toughest on drugs confirms that other parties are outdated and their policies are counterproductive. We need a new approach and fortunately there are ways forward.

In the UK, Green MP Caroline Lucas brought together a panel of experts to form the Brighton and Hove Independent Drugs Commission. Speaking in response to their report, she said: 'Drugs policy should be founded on the over-riding principle of reducing harm, both for users themselves and for wider society; any approach has to be led by the evidence about what works in practice.'[31]

Their recommendations sit within our existing legal framework and included:

- Significant expansion of the treatment Naloxone to counter the effects of opioid overdose, and 'First Aid for Overdose' training.

---

30 'Huge majority thinks "war on drugs" has failed, new poll finds', *The Observer*, 5 October 2014.

31 'Caroline thanks Brighton and Hove Independent Drugs Commission for groundbreaking work on drugs policy', 13 May 2014, www.carolinelucas.com/latest/ caroline-thanks-brighton-and-hove-independent-drugs-commission-for-groundbreaking-work-on, accessed 12 December 2014.

- Closer working between agencies in sharing information about drug-use patterns through participating in a Home Office-led Forensic Early Warning System.
- Pioneering work on reaching young people to educate on the dangers of drug and alcohol use.

Evidence from elsewhere in the world shows we can also go further in a radical policy shift that will take profits out of the underground economy and the control of drug dealers. In Colorado, an American state with a population of five million, taxation of legalised medicinal and recreational marijuana is now raising $7.5 million each month.[32] This is money that can then be used by the state to fund other medical services and programmes.

In California, where cannabis use has been decriminalised since January 2011, all of the risk areas associated with the policy decision have shown improvement.[33] Drug-based arrests are down by 23 per cent and property crime arrests are down by 25 per cent. Notably, school drop-out rates for 15–19-year-olds are down by 22 per cent.

In the UK, 36 per cent of the population have broken our existing laws in respect of using illegal drugs.[34] Every prosecution and police case that could be avoided if drugs were a medical rather than legal problem takes resources away from other issues. Every robbery committed to pay for drug addiction could be avoided if addicts didn't have to pay for treatment. It is the Greens who are in step with real public opinion and who will not subscribe to false moral outrage for the purposes of an election. There are financial costs to continuing a failed war on drugs and there are better ways to invest the tax that we pay.

---

32 'Colorado Marijuana Revenues Hit a New High', *Washington Post*, 14 October 2014.
33 'After California decriminalized marijuana, teen arrest, overdose and dropout rates fell', *Washington Post*, 15 October 2014.
34 European Monitoring Centre for Drugs and Drug Addiction.

Policing

Communities around the country have seen policing, fire and emergency services cuts at a local level for a number of years. The Greens want to see efficient and well-run government services, but the cuts that have been made in the age of austerity go way beyond any measure of efficiency. The 20 per cent cuts in the police budget since 2010 are having an impact on frontline policing.

There are cuts elsewhere that could be made instead of policing – Trident and HS2 are two hugely expensive areas of spending – but properly funded and trained police forces need to be paid for by general taxation. A fairer, more equal society would see lower crime rates and better funding for our public services. Even free market philosophers such as Robert Nozick want police to protect property rights. We see the role of police working in a positive way in communities extending far beyond that, but there is a lot of work to do.

For many communities, the police are not held in positive regard. The history since the MacPherson Report on the murder of Stephen Lawrence for the Metropolitan Police has not changed the perceptions. The disproportionate way in which stop-and-search targets black and Asian individuals divides the police from those communities. From my own work in deprived communities in Merseyside, there is also a problem in areas of social exclusion, where the fear of being labelled a 'grass' – and a fear of the consequences – creates a culture in which criminal activity ends up being tolerated in many areas. These are not 'quick fix' one-term issues. They require confidence-building and integration of police and the communities they serve. That requires investment in the future and not further cuts.

On the wider issues of policing and justice, the succession of revelations in relation to Hillsborough, child sexual abuse (CSA) and undercover infiltration has rightly raised deep concerns. At Hillsborough there was a systematic attempt to cover up, pass on blame and deny justice to the relatives of those Liverpool supporters who died. It has taken years for the truth to come out, with governments led by both of the largest parties guilty of dragging their feet. The exposure of Jimmy Savile's offences has subsequently revealed how cosy relations had been between a prolific, horrific abuser and the police. It's clear now that prosecutions are taking place, but the trust we place in our politicians, police and justice system is under scrutiny as never before.

Political engagement

The clear commitment of Green politicians to transparency, ethics and a better way of politics is needed now more than ever. We represent a real break from the British establishment. At a time when trust is low in our elected representatives and people are looking for hope in politics, for something better, the Greens represent that clean break from the past.

To suggest that any party or politician has the capacity to shape society alone is to fall into the hierarchical, top-down twentieth-century politics. We are in a new, more horizontal world in terms of access to information, posing a fundamental challenge to the traditional media, which is often owned by rich and powerful individuals with their own political views and agenda to shape. Facebook and Twitter have enabled middle-sized parties such as the Greens to challenge our exclusion and communicate our message to the public. The *Why Vote* series is a more traditional format, but will be tweeted and liked by thousands. If people are online daily, on their phones and tablets, and they are informed about the decisions that are being made on their behalf, they can and will be engaged in that process. Electing 650 people, who will be mostly men, to a Parliament to make representative decisions, is an entirely different process in the early twenty-first century.

Politics needs to move with the times. We need active citizens who are engaged in the process of politics in Britain. The Scottish referendum has shown just what is possible when people can understand

and discuss key issues. We can do more of this and we should have confidence in the decisions that the people of this country can make. There should be more referenda. In Switzerland, voters rejected overwhelmingly the case for extremely tight immigration rules.[35] We must have confidence in modern political engagement and the power of our technology to reach people with messages that challenge and overturn those interests which have dominated our society for the last 100 years.

The radicalism we propose, not just in domestic affairs, but in proposing real redistribution of wealth and a profoundly different foreign policy, will have powerful opponents. Our policies for them may provoke fear and will be resisted by those who think they know better than the people of our country. They will not succeed. Green policies are already the most popular of any party on the Vote for Policies website.

Our role at the election is to turn that support to Green votes and to build a Britain that in fifty years' time will be proudly diverse. The Green arguments that we can build a fairer society, that immigration is not a crime and that all people, not just those who have disproportionate power, should shape our future, will succeed in 21st-century Britain. Now it's over to you as voters to make it happen.

Peter Cranie is an anti-racism campaigner who has stood as the Green's European candidate for the North West region. He works as a lecturer covering education, social care and public services. @PeterCranie

---

35   'Ecopop referendum: Swiss reject immigration curbs', BBC Online.

Chapter 8

Young People and Politics

AMELIA WOMACK

It is often said 'young people are the future'. Indeed they are – they will be the people that we rely on to pay tax, build our communities and make decisions that will affect our lives; some of us will soon be relying upon them to create the capital that feeds our pension scheme. Yet young people are also our present; they represent 20 per cent of our current population – and they are desperately try- ing to survive the brunt of the cuts. Cuts that have been created by politicians they didn't elect due to a lack of inspiration and belief that there is anything worth voting for, resulting in just 44 per cent of 18–24-year-olds and just 55 per cent of 25–34-year-olds voting in the 2010 general election.[36]

These statistics inspire another popular phrase – that young people just aren't interested in politics. This is often said to justify ignoring them. However, it's not young people who aren't interested in poli- tics, but politicians who aren't interested in young people.

In this chapter, we shall see how the Green Party is ensuring that we have robust policies to support this 'present generation', to ensure that they have the knowledge, skills and opportunities to create a thriving generation ready to meet the challenges of the future.

---

36 'How Britain Voted in 2010,' Ipsos MORI, 21 May 2010.

Voter turnout

The biggest challenge with regard to young people is low voter turn-out and representation. In the election for European Parliament in 2014, a number of groups offered training to 'young' candidates. Now, although it is traditionally people under thirty or under thirty-five who are considered young, this training was offered to candidates under forty – because the under-forties are under-represented and don't vote. So, will this 'apathetic generation' that politicians talk about end, or will it simply become an apathetic population?

This lack of engagement at the ballot box is poignant because young people have historically been central to political activism all round the world. They fought for suffrage and the fall of the Berlin Wall; they marched against the Iraq War; and, in 2010, they were key to the 50,000-strong protest against tuition fees. It's important for us to recognise that political participation means so much more than simply voting. It also covers active forms of politics including sign-ing petitions, attending protests, creating viral social media waves against inequality, campaigning and even occupation.

Notice the official hypocrisy shown during the recent Occupy Democracy protests. The government supported the pro-democracy demonstrations in Hong Kong while forbidding peaceful pro-democracy demonstrations to happen here. This expression of democracy on Parliament Square in London was met with a barrage of police and forty arrests for such acts as 'sitting on a piece of tarpaulin', 'using sound amplification equipment', 'playing musical instruments', and even 'sitting on pizza boxes'. A number of our members were arrested, including Jenny Jones. The average age of arrestees was approximately twenty-eight.[37] These young people were engaging in democratic political action, and the Green Party was in full support – but the government treated them like criminals.

We need to be shifting the discussion away from the idea of an

37   *Regina* vs *Pete Kennedy*, London, 2014.

apathetic generation, because young people are probably as political now as they ever have been, and are engaged in new forms of politics, from activism to social media to tarpaulin to Twitter. We need to be talking about how we make politics something that we are all involved in, rather than something that is done to us, and we need to ensure that our voices are heard.

Why don't young people turn out to vote? Well, the biggest reason is that they don't trust political parties. Research has shown that approximately 75 per cent of young people distrust politicians.[38] This mistrust is no surprise, given government U-turns and a raft of policies negatively affecting young people. Tuition fees have been a prime example. Despite 2001 election promises, the Labour Party increased top-up fees of up to £3,000 a year. In response to this, the Liberal Democrats made scrapping tuition fees one of their fundamental pledges of their 2010 election campaign. Young people and students turned out in droves to vote for the Liberal Democrats, but were let down on a colossal scale when the Liberal Democrats voted to *treble* tuition fees to £9,000 in 2012 – creating the most expensive education system in Europe, and a system that is fundamentally broken.

This betrayal by the Liberal Democrats has deeply affected an entire generation of young voters. It also seems deeply hypocritical that *all* the MPs who voted to triple tuition fees had either received free higher education or paid, at worst, £1,000 tuition fees. Society made the investment in the education of these people so that they could go on to contribute to the economy, pay taxes and be active participants in our society. Yet now, our MPs have abandoned this and we have a generation of young people who are leaving university with a degree, £45,000 of debt, and one of the toughest job markets of the last hundred years. The Green Party rejects the unfairness of this intergenerational inequality and would restore free education and end the tyranny of tuition fees. Fees that young people on lower

38   L. Bouza, 'Addressing Youth Absenteeism in the European Elections', European Youth Forum, Brussels, 2014.

wages are so busy paying off that they have very little left to consider paying into a retirement fund. Considering the future of pensions – this is a time bomb just waiting to go off.

Citizen's income

The Green Party would also support all members of society through the introduction of a basic income. The basic income is a regular unconditional payment of money, much like child benefit, to all citizens. This income would not only ensure that students can finance themselves through university and concentrate on their studies, but also plug the gap created by the scrapping of the educational maintenance allowance (EMA). This cut led to a reduction of 8,000 in the number of people accessing education and means that young people from more advantaged neighbourhoods are now three times more likely to enter higher education than those from disadvantaged ones. The Green Party's passion for education galvanised Young Greens to organise the 2014 free education march attended by over 5,000 young people. The march called for a free education for everyone and the reintroduction of EMA to ensure no one's right to education is compromised by lack of finance.

Youth services

Outside of school, young people have faced coalition cuts to youth services that have torn the very fabric of our communities – 2,000 youth service jobs and more than 350 youth centres were obliterated between 2012 and 2014.[39] These institutions not only give young people a place to work on new projects and develop skills, but also

---

39   M. Leftly, 'Cuts to youth services "will lead to poverty and crime", say unions', *The Independent*, 10 August 2014, www.independent.co.uk/news/uk/politics/cuts-to-youth-services-will-lead-to-poverty-and-crime-say-unions-9659504.html, accessed 12 January 2015.

provide career advice for young people and a safe space to explore their own identities. These cuts have once again disproportionately affected young people from poorer backgrounds and Unison members working in youth services believe that these cuts are also a catalyst for higher youth unemployment.

Cuts to youth services are short-sighted. With little support and feeling isolated, many desperate young people could turn to a life of crime. The Audit Commission has stated that a young person in the criminal system costs the taxpayer more than £200,000 per year. When giving young people support in the form of leisure activities, careers advice etc. costs £50,000, by comparison, then it is evident that investment in young people not only provides a more flourishing society, but also saves the taxpayer money.

Politics needs to aspire to address social and environmental externalities such as these. The Green Party pledges to increase youth expenditure to £1 billion and to create 2,000 young people's centres, ensuring that young people are supported outside of education.

Brighton Green Party runs one of the few councils to still provide youth services in-house, and has done so by utilising a 'one-stop shop'. This has made Brighton & Hove one of the most improved areas in England, with only 6.6 per cent of 16–18-year-olds not in employment, education or training, compared to the 13.1 per cent across the UK.[40]

On top of these cuts, one of the biggest injustices of the current system is that once graduates find themselves in the world of work, saddled with debt, most will have to complete one or more internships to get their foot on the employment ladder. With one-third of internships unpaid, this system only benefits young people who can live with their parents in a location where there are jobs available

---

40   J. M. Davies, 'NEET: Young People Not in Education, Employment or Training – Commons Library Standard Note', 20 November 2014, www.parliament.uk/business/publications/research/briefing-papers/SN06705/neet-young-people-not-in-education-employment-or-training, accessed 12 January 2015.

(generally a big city), or those whose parents can afford to pay their living costs while they complete an internship. In addition, many internships do not result in paid work, nor provide any fulfilling training to get you onto the career ladder. Internships can cost an individual up to £926 per month in London or £804 in Manchester – yet the company benefits from the added value for a period of three to six months.

This unjust system only benefits the rich and 70 per cent of the population believes that these internships are 'unfair'. The Green Party believes that anyone in employment should be paid at least the living wage, and elected Greens in the European Parliament have been tirelessly campaigning to ensure employers provide paid internships with quality training, development and potential employment.

They have also taken on the battle against Workfare with 'Youth Guarantee' system. This ensures that young people who have been on Jobseekers' Allowance for more than four months are entitled to training, education or work, rather than being forced to work unpaid for big corporations – an employment strategy that is fundamentally not fit for society.

Employment

Young people not only have a less secure education, but also a less secure working environment. Research from the Joseph Rowntree Foundation highlights the sharp increase in the number of under-25s living in poverty due to the increase of insecure employment such as zero-hours contracts.[41] These contracts allow businesses to hire people, without providing any workers' rights or guaranteed hours. The insecure nature of these contracts has seen landlords refusing to accept tenants who are working on these contracts. While

---

41   T. McInnes et al., 'Monitoring Poverty and Social Exclusion 2014', Joseph Rowntree Foundation, 24 November 2014, www.jrf.org.uk/publications/monitoring-poverty-and-social-exclusion-2014, accessed 12 January 2015.

talking to young people, I have discovered that many of them can hold up to three of these contracts, and still not make ends meet. The Green Party campaigns to ban these callous contracts in favour of flexible, part-time or full-time contracts that meet our workers' rights and a living wage.

To add to this strife, the safety net that our country has provided to protect the most vulnerable has been ripped out from under the feet of young people. The Conservative and Labour parties have announced that they would cut benefits for 18–21-year-olds. Young people are already the victims of austerity cuts: over 52 per cent of those seeking help with homelessness are under the age of twenty-five.[42]

Given the state of the economic climate as well as the barriers to education and work, austerity cuts at the final safety rope for young people. No wonder young people don't feel that turning up to vote will do anything to change their futures, and for some that future is looking increasingly bleak.

Actions needed

With all of these issues affecting every aspect of young people's lives, the language of change is important. The Scottish referendum proved how change can wake up the youth vote, with engagement as high as 80 per cent. It highlights that when young people have a real chance to vote for change, they get out and vote.[43] Scottish Young Green co-chair Zara Kitson said, 'This is an opportunity of a generation ... an opportunity of being a part of building my country.' Isn't that what politics and voting should be about? A clear way to

---

42 www.homeless.org.uk/connect/news/2014/nov/19/missed-opportunity-to-prevent-youth-homelessness, accessed 9 January 2015.

43 A. McSmith, 'Scottish referendum results: Huge turnout bolsters case for voting at 16,' *The Independent*, 19 September 2014, www.independent.co.uk/news/uk/scottish-independence/scottish-referendum-results-huge-turnout-bolsters-case-for-voting-at-16-9745081.html, accessed 12 January 2015.

influence decision-making to build the vision of the country you want to be a part of.

Only 55 per cent of all 18–24-year-olds are registered to vote (compared to 94 per cent of over-65s). If all of them registered to vote, their sheer numbers would wake politicians up to the need for strong youth policies. We can show politicians that we are ready to use our power and change the face of British politics. There wouldn't just be an earthquake at the ballot boxes, but politicians would make greater effort to speak to youth – making pledges that benefit this generation. It's time that politics met the needs of this new generation of voters rather than have politicians chasing only the grey vote.

To communicate opportunities and empower young people, we need to rise above the political language barrier. The put-downs, attempts to get the upper hand and jeering in the Commons bear no relation to anything most people can relate to. It's like a new language – and one that is purposely designed to ensure that only a certain elite group can take part in the conversations that will change the future of our country. The language is so isolating and irrelevant to many young people they may as well just start conducting parliamentary debates in Latin. Our generation is the first generation to have grown up with a completely televised Parliament – something that should support engagement – yet it has simply laid bare the failings of our current political system. To address this, the Young Greens create a youth manifesto for every election, something that no other party provides, as a tool to tackle youth apathy. In addition, we empower our young people and improve their confidence by providing training with the Thirty under Thirty programme. This programme provides a year of training for thirty Young Greens to ensure that they achieve their full potential within the party, and has been providing us with some inspirational Young Green figures.

In addition, inspiration through representation impacts participation. By having young people at the highest levels of politics and political institutions we can not only inspire young people but also ensure that there is a youth voice. It can be argued that no Parliament or political organisation is legitimate if young people are not a part of it.[44] The importance of this has been recognised in the Green Party's constitution by having our elected Young Green co-chairs also serve on the national governing body.

We campaign to inspire young voters through championing votes at sixteen. It is widely acknowledged that not only is this important to engage more young people, but is fundamental to democracy itself. With the current system a sixteen-year-old could be paying tax, joining the army, and having a child, yet not have any say about who is making decisions on their working life, the wars the army fights or the decisions that affect their future and that of their children.

Even more frustrating than the situation for sixteen-year-olds is for those people who are nearly eighteen on the day of a general election. These unlucky people will be almost twenty-three before they are given any say in who should govern the country.

The next general election will be the most important election we have witnessed, and we need to ensure that all voices are represented. Yet young people have another barrier to break through since changes in voter registration could mean that more youth votes are eliminated from the 2015 general election. This election will see the UK move to individual electoral registration, whereupon voters will now register individually rather than for the whole household. When this was introduced in Northern Ireland, the youth vote dropped significantly due to universities being unable to register them. Unless we break the barriers to young people voting we shall devalue our own democracy. The Green Party is currently working with Young Green groups to get many young people registered, but it's unlikely that its efforts will secure the same numbers of young people registered as there were in 2010.

All of these policies, actions and case studies prove that the Green

---

44   I. f. D. a. E. A. (IDEA), 'Youth Participation in Politics and Elections', 2013.

Party believes that young people should be central to any vision of the future. However, we haven't created these policies to 'capture the youth vote' but because they are right. These policies have been created, costed and developed by our members, and in most cases created by young people for young people. These policies are fundamental to our present young generation, who are currently building their paths in society and, as a result, these policies have attracted a 400 per cent increase in Young Green membership within six months this year – 20 per cent of the national party. In addition, polls consistently say that approximately 28 per cent of 18–24-year-olds and 14 per cent of 25–34-year-olds will be voting Green in 2015.

In the case of the Green Party, politicians are interested in young people and, as a result, young people are becoming interested in politics.

Amelia Womack became deputy leader of the Green Party in 2014 at the age of twenty-nine. Her work with the League of Young Voters during the European elections inspired her to campaign on youth issues. @Amelia_Womack

Chapter 9

Constitutional Reform

ADAM RAMSAY

Hierarchy

When power concentrates in the hands of the few, so does wealth. It shouldn't be surprising, therefore, that the country with the least democratic constitutional set-up in the Western world is also one of its most financially unequal countries. That country, of course, is Britain.

Some of the elitisms of the British constitution are well known: the House of Lords, the power of the monarchy, first-past-the-post, and the astounding proportion of our MPs who are men. On these issues, Greens are clear.

The fact that one of the two chambers of our Parliament is largely appointed by the leaders of our main parties means that lines of patronage are wrapped around the neck of our democracy. The House of Lords must be abolished and replaced with an elected chamber. Similarly, every baby born this year should have the same chances in life as every other. There is no place for the hereditary principle in the modern era. That means it's time to abolish the monarchy.

First-past-the-post has never really been democratic enough, but in the modern world of multi-party politics it must be replaced with a system that ensures our representatives reflect who we want

to vote for, not those whom a few people in a few marginal constituencies want to keep out. We must have a voting system which
allocates MPs to parties in proportion to how many votes they get.
The increasingly multi-party nature of our democracy makes this
more important than ever.

It is vital too that our representatives are just that – that they
represent the diversity of the people of this country. If anything,
marginalised groups should have more access to power now, in order
to even out the imprints of histories of oppression felt across society.
And yet in reality, Westminster in particular and electoral politics
in general are significantly more male and significantly more white
than the British population.

To fix this, parties must lead from the front. It is therefore telling
that, of the ten parliamentary or assembly seats held by Greens across
the UK, six are held by women and only two are held by straight,
white men. Of the nine leaders, deputy leaders and co-conveners
of the Green Parties of England, Wales, Northern Ireland and Scotland, five are women and only two are straight, white men. No other
party can match this.

But ensuring our representation is as diverse as our population
will take more than the Green Party setting a good example. Westminster is one of the worst places for female representation in the
democratic world. Many of the rules of the place come from a time
when MPs were all rich men, so it's no wonder those are the people
who find it easiest to work there today.

When Caroline Lucas arrived at the Palace of Westminster having just been elected as the first Green MP, she was shown not to
her office, but to a pink ribbon 'on which to hang her sword'. Having spent a decade in the European Parliament, she was horrified by
the relic she found in London. She has highlighted a list of simple
ways that parliamentary procedure could change which would make
it more possible for ordinary people to represent us there, including
allowing MPs to job share, making it easier for people with caring

responsibilities to carry out their role, and ending late-night voting so that it's possible to be an MP and have a family life. More radically, the long-standing Green policy of providing everyone with a basic income on which to live would allow for many more to be actively engaged in politics at every level.

It's not just by making Parliament more inclusive that our politics will be changed. As long as it's possible for the rich and powerful to buy influence, our journey to democracy will be incomplete. In the year after the 2010 general election, in the shadow of the biggest financial crisis in nearly a century, 51.4 per cent of donations to the Conservative Party came from the City of London.[45] Is it any wonder they still haven't cracked down on Britain's dangerous finance sector? It was revealed in 2014 that private companies with links to Tory MPs had received £1.5 billion in privatised NHS contracts and that tax-dodging experts PricewaterhouseCoopers have given the Labour party £600,000 of consultancy time to 'help' write their tax policies.[46] If it feels like public policy in Britain is written by big business for big business, then that's no coincidence.

In fact, PricewaterhouseCoopers is one of many companies said by Channel 4's FactCheck to have a 'revolving door' with the government and political parties – allowing them to help write the rules, before going back to jobs advising the mega-rich and big businesses on how to get round the rules they've just written.[47] One of the prominent figures on PwC's staff is former Labour Secretary of State for Health Alan Milburn – one of the ministers key to accelerating the privatisation of the NHS. He oversees their healthcare practice, allowing him to cash in on a system he helped to set up.[48]

45   www.theguardian.com/politics/2011/sep/30/city-conservatives-donations, accessed 12 December 2014.

46   www.theguardian.com/politics/2014/nov/12/pricewaterhousecoopers-tax-structures-politics-influence, accessed 12 December 2014.

47   blogs.channel4.com/factcheck/whitehalls-revolving-doors-factcheck-qa/13596, accessed 12 December 2014.

48   www.opendemocracy.net/ournhs/caroline-molloy/milburn-nhs-and-britains-revolving-door, accessed 12 December 2014.

This isn't a one-off. As the journalist George Monbiot has summa-
rised, many of the committees making vital decisions about how we
are governed are staffed by employees or recent employees of companies who stand to benefit to the tune of billions from the decisions
they are making.[49] Greens have a long track record of standing up
to vested interests rather than inviting them into the heart of government; of fighting privatisation, and of openness in governance,
with Britain's Green MEPs scoring high in transparency rankings.[50]

Some of the worst things about the way Britain is run are those
which are less talked about: the Crown Protectorates and British
Overseas Territories form the biggest network of tax havens and
secrecy areas in the world, depriving vital public services here and
across the planet of hundreds of trillions of pounds.[51] British local
government is really just a wing of central government, rather than
a dynamic force in its own right; 'parliamentary sovereignty' means
that power in our country flows from Westminster down, when it
should rise up from the people.

People's constitution

One of the most extraordinary things about the British constitution
is that there isn't really one – or, rather, there isn't a codified one.
Other than Israel, Saudi Arabia and New Zealand, no other country
on earth lacks any such formal control on the power of the powerful. And this causes real problems. It allowed Margaret Thatcher to
abolish the Greater London Authority and the Lothian and Strath-
clyde regional councils when they stood up to her. It means our rights
aren't properly enshrined, allowing the government to ban protest

---

49   www.theguardian.com/commentisfree/2012/mar/12/nhs-health, accessed 12 Decem-
      ber 2014.

50   www.greenparty.org.uk/news/2009-05-25-open-europe.html, accessed 12 December
      2014.

51   www.theguardian.com/business/2013/nov/07/britain-tax-havens-queen-secrecy-jus-
      tice-network, accessed 12 December 2014.

within sight of Parliament and to spy on us when we use the internet. It means the rules by which we are governed are made up as they go along, and can always be bent to the will of those in power.

Greens support the introduction of a written constitution in Britain. This constitution should be penned not by the government, but by a convention of the people. There are examples from across the world and from some of our nearest neighbours from which much can be learnt, with both Ireland and Iceland having held similar processes in recent years.

The process of writing such a constitution would allow for Britain not just to fix the problems listed, but to learn from best practice across the world – and to lead it. It would allow us to give sixteen- and seventeen-year-olds the vote, introduce rules so we can recall politicians who breach our trust, follow Namibia and Bolivia in introducing constitutional protections for the natural world and discuss how we can use new technology to facilitate more direct democracy. It provides a vital opportunity to rip power from the grip of Westminster and bring it closer to our communities.

It is exactly this desire to decentralise power which was on display in the biggest constitutional debate of our generation – the Scottish referendum. The Scottish Green Party were vocal and passionate supporters of a 'Yes' vote, and Greens in England and Wales stood shoulder to shoulder with them. Too often, the Westminster parties claim that they want to bring power closer to people. But when push came to shove – when they realised that giving power to people meant losing it themselves – they united like never before behind a status quo which leaves them in charge. Waving Union flags, they dismissed those who thought they could run their country better than the crisis-ridden British state as 'petty nationalists'.

Greens backed a 'Yes' vote because it meant bringing power closer to people, because it gave the people of Scotland the chance to escape our broken Westminster system, and because it presented an opportunity to win radical reforms for people across the rest of the UK.

After all, ours is one of the most unequal countries in the Western world – it wouldn't be hard to do things better.

In the week before the referendum, as the polls got closer, people all across the UK saw the look of fear in the eyes of our rulers. And it's important to remember that, because it's a reminder that, ultimately, it's the people of this country who have power. And the panic amongst the elite meant that the window for change isn't entirely shut – it remains open for us all.

Decentralisation

Over-centralisation doesn't just impact on Scotland. It must be addressed all across the UK. This is why Greens believe in handing significantly more control to local authorities, so that decisions about our lives are made somewhere we can easily get to when we want to influence them, and so we can ensure they are the right choices for our different communities. And it's why Greens support proposals for regional assemblies. Devolution has been a massive success in Scotland and Wales, and there's no reason why Yorkshire, the north-west or Cornwall shouldn't benefit hugely from it too.

Devolution is the wrong word. Power shouldn't be handed down from Westminster. It belongs to us, the people. We allow representatives to exercise it on our behalf because sometimes that's the best way to work together. But sometimes we should be able to take decisions ourselves. Because we're the people who know our communities best.

In the Leith area of Edinburgh, because of work done by Scottish Green Party co-convener and councillor Maggie Chapman, people are beginning to do just that. She and the other councillors from around Leith were given money to allocate to local community projects. But rather than make decisions on behalf of the community, Maggie persuaded them to hand that power directly to the community. And so they organised an event for people from the area to come together and choose how to spend the money themselves. Now, every year, thousands of people in Leith get together, hear from each group of their neighbours that wants the cash in order to make things better in their area – an impoverished part of Edinburgh – and decide how to allocate the funding.

As well as ensuring that the people who know the area best are the people who make decisions about it, these events have had another side effect: they have helped to build community. They have brought the various community groups together, along with thousands of locals. And it's not just through participatory budgeting that Greens believe in putting power back into the hands of people. It's not a coincidence that the only council administration in England to propose a referendum so residents could vote on whether to save local services by paying a little more council tax is the only Green Party minority administration: Brighton. And it's a measure of the distaste for democracy amongst the other parties that Labour and the Tories teamed up to veto this vote.

As Westminster has pulled political power away from our communities, we've had fewer and fewer chances to engage with our neighbours in how to run our areas. Greens will fight to bring that power back through participatory budgeting, local referendums and other forms of direct democracy. It's not because Greens know your area better than you do that you should vote for them, but because they understand that they don't. You and your neighbours know best.

Too often, politicians and journalists dismiss us, the citizens of this country, as apathetic. This is utter bunkum. Of course we care about our friends and our families and our neighbours – and people at the other end of the country and on the other side of the world. The problem isn't that we don't care. It's that our system is set up in a way which makes it almost impossible to change anything. And so many of us have given up trying, turned off the news, and got on with our lives. By bringing power much, much closer to people, by putting us back in charge of our communities, Greens will unleash a new democratic revolution in Britain.

And it's not just by centralising power that politicians have made it hard for us to have a say about our future, because the main shift in power in the last few decades has been the rise of corporate control. Too often, Westminster has ripped power from communities, and then handed it to some multinational or other. It's no wonder so few of us vote. Elections used to give us a say over how our trains were run, the level of rent we paid, the way our electricity was distributed and how our telephones worked. Now these questions are answered not through a conversation between the people, but by the global markets.

We've ended up with some of the most expensive and worst-run trains in Europe, some of the lowest levels of renewable energy use in the EU (despite having the highest potential) ... I could go on. It's no coincidence that when you hand decisions about the utilities and services we all use to the rich and powerful, they choose to run things in ways that maximise profits for them by charging us a fortune to squash into a crowded train, racking our rent up while failing to fix the boiler and running our energy system as though there's literally no tomorrow.

So, for Greens, these are constitutional questions too, because they are about who has power in our society: the 1 per cent or the 99 per cent. Like most people in Britain, we think our basic utilities should be brought back under public control. Privatisation was an experiment and, by any sensible measure, it has failed. We need to bring power to the people. In some cases, that means renationalisation. But often it will mean cooperatives, local authority ownership and mutuals. From banking to energy, the free market model has failed us, and we need the set-up of our country to be designed around our basic needs, not maximising corporate profit.

Europe

While we want to bring power as close to people as possible, sometimes decisions can't be made at the level of a neighbourhood. As global corporations try to divide workers in a race to the bottom, as fish stocks in the North Sea dwindle, as global problems from antibiotic resistance to climate change get ever more serious, we need international structures.

For that reason, Greens think it's worth trying to make the EU work. Unlike Labour and the Lib Dems, we are under no illusions about its current success: for every workers' right it has protected (and there are many) there is an EU–US trade deal handing huge powers to global corporations. There are huge advantages to the free movement of people across the continent, but huge disadvantages to the fact that we can no longer restrict capital flows when we need to. The EU has brought peace to our continent, but the trade deals it has imposed on Africa, Asia and Latin America have entrenched poverty in some of the poorest areas of the earth. Greens have always said that the Euro won't work, and it hasn't.

But we are used to political structures that fail us. Leaving the EU wouldn't bring power to communities in Britain. It would just hand control to Westminster – and it would mean chucking in the best chance we have of proper co-operation across our continent, making it harder for us to stand up to corporations in our globalised world.

The reforms David Cameron wants are exactly the wrong ones: he wants an EU that's run for the 1 per cent, where companies can up and leave a community any time they want but we aren't allowed to move if that's the best way to get a job or live with a loved one. He wants an EU which doesn't properly regulate our banks but does have the right to sell off our NHS on the global market. We want the opposite of that.

But if we're going to build that EU, then it will take work. Another Europe is possible, but only if the people of Britain and the people of Europe are ready to stand up to our rulers and make it happen. And so the Green Party thinks it should be up to the people to decide if we are going to stay in the EU. We support a referendum on Europe, we will campaign to stay in, and we will work to build a movement for a Europe that's run for people and planet, not profit.

More democracy

For forty years now, power has been concentrated ever more in the hands of the powerful – within the UK, and across the globe. When a group of protesters set up camp on the steps of St Paul's and declared that the world is run not by and for the people, but by and for the 1 per cent, they had it right. Too often, commentators think that the crisis in 2008 was about simple economics. But, in truth, it was much more than that. Because, while the economic impacts are vast, they were the symptom. And as long as we respond with only macro-economic answers – whether the right ones or the wrong ones, they will not be enough.

In practice, the 2008 banking crisis was caused by the same thing as the expenses scandal, as the phone-hacking scandal, as the child sex abuse horrors still being uncovered, as our disastrous foreign policy in the Middle East ... we have allowed power to become unaccountable. We have put too much control over our communities into the hands of too few people.

Even if they had the best of intentions, no one small clique would ever on their own be able to run a country in the complex modern world. More democracy is needed to ensure that every point of view is seen and every angle heard. But, in practice, the intentions of those who run the country aren't always the best. In practice, our rulers are too good at conning themselves into believing that their self-interest is the same thing as the interest of all of us. In practice, the power we have allowed a small elite to accumulate is too often being abused.

This has to change. It's up to the people of this country to make it change. The political parties who have become intertwined with this system won't be able to do that job for us. And so we need to elect to

Westminster representatives from parties not bound into the status quo. We need to elect politicians whose aim is to bring power back to us – people from a party which has radical democracy as one of its founding principles. And that means voting Green.

Adam Ramsay is co-editor of the UK section of openDemocracy.net, author of 42 Reasons to Support Scottish Independence and is involved in various activist groups, but his opinions are his own. @AdamRamsay

Chapter 10

Housing

TOM CHANCE

Like many people my age, I've been evicted from my home because I stood up for my rights. My first landlord after moving to London would probably be called a 'rogue landlord' today. He left the property in a damp condition, concealed his real identity from us, and tried to withhold our deposit. When our boiler broke down he sent one of his unqualified mates to try and fix it, but this mate was unable to provide a CORGI certificate (now the Gas Safe Register), so we refused him entry. As soon as he was able, the landlord terminated our Assured Shorthold Tenancy and booted us out.

Most people I know who are under the age of thirty-five still rent privately, unable to afford to buy a home or qualify for social housing. They're angry about it, and fed up with the insecurity, the high costs, and the poor-quality homes they have to put up with. But only 56 per cent of private tenants in England are registered to vote, compared to 87 per cent of homeowners.

Why are almost half of renters not even bothering to register so that they can vote in politicians who could do something to improve their lives? One reason is that it's difficult to stay registered when you have to move every six or twelve months. When you've just had to contact your mobile phone provider, your bank, the student loan company and half a dozen other companies to tell them of your new address, trying to find the correct form to send your council falls off the to-do list.

But I think a deeper reason is that they don't see the point. Who could they vote for that understands their plight and has real solutions to offer? What do we ever hear from politicians on the evening news, or read from them in the national newspapers? Grey party leaders intone: there is a housing crisis, it's terribly important, and we will build lots of new homes to sort it out. We have heard this same message for years, and yet the problems persist and nobody connects with the feelings of people left behind.

The anger of my fellow renting young professionals is as nothing compared to the anger of council tenants being forced out of their neighbourhoods by demolition and gentrification. Why should these tenants be cheered by the 'build more homes' mantra when those homes are all too often luxury flats built on the land where their council homes used to stand?

Our despair at not being able to buy a home is as nothing compared to the despair of single parents forced to relocate to another side of the country because of benefit cuts, made worse by the victimisation of 'scroungers' on our TV screens and in every tabloid newspaper. Every time a grey politician promises to 'get tough' on the tiny minority of benefit cheats, the victimised majority of people who need benefits to make ends meet know they are in for another wave of cuts to their weekly budget. What will go next – the heating, the cups of tea, the TV on a weekly rental?

We are all fed up with this malaise, as are the parents whose children can't move out, the villagers unable to stop 'executive homes' being built on prime agricultural farmland, and – if they had a voice we might learn this too – the animals and insects and plants on brownfield and greenfield sites that are trashed without any consideration for their importance are probably fed up as well. If I were asked by any of these people, 'why should I register to vote Green?', I would say: because we are the only party that wants to bring you hope.

To understand why, I'm afraid we need to go back into the bad
news stories, because one of the distinctive things about the Green
Party is our desire to get to the root of the problem and fix that,
rather than fiddling around in the upper branches of a diseased tree.

How homes became so unaffordable

This crisis has unfolded over decades. Relative to other prices,
house prices have gone up five-fold since 1955. In less than twenty
years the price of houses has doubled relative to incomes. The
problem really spiralled out of control in the last fifteen years.
House price inflation averaged 11 per cent between 1997 and 2007,
and prices have never fallen back to an affordable level relative to
incomes in spite of the recession.

As a consequence, the average income of first-time buyers has
almost doubled since the early 1980s. In London, where these statistics are always more extreme, 80 per cent of the new-build sales
market is affordable to only 20 per cent of working households, and
the average first-time buyer is now in the top 20 per cent of London's
household income distribution.

You sometimes read newspaper columnists saying it's all the fault
of young people who go on too many holidays or buy too many
clothes. If only they saved like I did, the columnist laments, they'd
be able to buy a home. This response, now thankfully becoming quite
rare, just makes people even more angry and frustrated. Back in 1971
it was really quite expensive to go on holiday and buy new clothes, but
comparatively cheap to buy a home. Today the situation has reversed,
with cheap holidays but impossibly expensive homes.

Anybody who downplays the affordability problem needs to take a
long, hard look at those numbers. The campaign group Shelter has a
nice way of making this a bit more real. If grocery prices had increased
at the same rate as house prices since 1971, then a four-pint carton
of milk would now cost £10, a bunch of six bananas would cost £8

and a loaf of sliced white bread would cost £4. Maybe the columnists would take note if their breakfast was that pricey?

Over the same period, the number of social rented homes in the
UK actually fell. The term 'social rented' is a catch-all for homes
provided by councils, housing associations and some co-ops, giving
genuinely affordable rents and secure tenancies to those unable to
get by in the private housing market. In 1981 there were 5.5 million
social rented homes in England, but twenty years later we only had
4 million, despite the total number of households in the country rising by a third. As home ownership remained stagnant then fell, and
the stock of social housing was eroded, most people found themselves renting privately instead.

The causes of this deterioration in the affordability of housing are
complex, but at the most basic level there were three problems created by Labour and Conservative governments over the past thirty
or forty years: the sale and demolition of social housing, the failure
to build enough new homes of the right type, and the refusal to tax
housing and land properly.

Selling off the family silver

In the 1970s, various Labour and Conservative politicians floated the
idea that council tenants should be able to buy their home. To some
it sounded like a great idea – it would help them to own an asset
which they can borrow against, to take control of their life, and so
on. Others thought it was a deliberate attempt to tie working-class
people to mortgages, so they would be reluctant to go on strike for
fear of defaulting and losing their home.

When Thatcher's government introduced the policy, called Right
to Buy, it set in motion one of the largest privatisations in British
history. Council tenants were given discounts on the homes, a massive subsidy to people who would in time come to be quite wealthy
because of the value of their home. More than 2 million homes were

sold off, the money was hoovered up by central government, and no replacement homes were built.

This policy continued under the Major government. Blair's New Labour left it alone, not wanting to frighten off the aspiring classes. Brown at least increased the social housing budget when he was Chancellor of the Exchequer to build more new social rented homes, which led to the stock stabilising in recent years. But even he wasn't willing to scrap this firesale of the family silver.

Other council homes were sold at auctions or demolished. You'd expect some of this to go on as a good way to manage the stock, but not on the scale we have seen. The worst excesses of demolition have come through regeneration schemes. Some of the most noto-rious have been in northern cities, where entire streets like Welsh Street in Liverpool were boarded up and left empty by Labour gov-ernments, and in London, where successful estates like the Heygate in Elephant & Castle were demonised and then demolished to make way for luxury flats built by private developers.

Council tenants campaigning against these policies became lonely voices in the wilderness, largely ignored by the three grey parties, who continued to talk in bland and deceitful generalities about the need to build more homes. The result is that we now have millions of low-income households renting privately and 1.5 million in Eng-land claiming housing benefit at a cost of over £8 billion a year. That's compared to just over £1 billion a year that the government spends on building new affordable homes (many of which aren't even very affordable).

A clean Green break for tenants

But the Green Party has long promoted a set of policies that would break with this forty-year consensus against social housing. We would scrap the Right to Buy, substantially increase the social housing budget so that we could build enough homes within a generation to meet all needs, and refurbish and improve homes and estates.

Don't let that make you think that Green politics is about harkening back to a mythical golden age, or about trying to be the Old Labour that Blair and Brown abandoned. We also have some bright ideas to make the future even better. For example, in place of 'Right to Buy' we would introduce a 'Right to Rent' for homeowners struggling with their mortgage. If you were close to defaulting, you could sell your home to your local council and rent it back on a secure tenancy, with the option of buying it back again when you have your finances in order again. That way you can stay in your home instead of having it repossessed. It completely upends the Right to Buy idea, and makes council housing a solution for homeowners.

We also want to democratise council housing and housing associations, giving tenants much more control over their homes and neighbourhoods. We want to support more people to start housing co-operatives, which are a mainstream type of housing in places like Scandinavia and Canada.

All of our policies in this area would re-assert the basic principle that everybody has a right to affordable, secure and comfortable accommodation.

Those luxury apartments and executive homes

Most housing campaign groups like Shelter, the National Housing Federation and PricedOut say that the single most important solution to our problems is building more homes. They often single out objectors as the main obstacle to this solution. The stereotypes sound compelling – the comfortable NIMBY who moved into a new home in a village and now wants to stop any more being built next door; the misguided green who goes on about protecting farmland when we haven't been self-sufficient for well over a century; the self-interested homeowner who rather likes the value of their price rising and doesn't want new homes to stop that. But they are sometimes guilty of ignoring or underplaying some legitimate reasons people have for opposing new housing being built. Here are a few.

New homes have a bad reputation in the UK for being small and pokey, with no storage space and gloomy rooms. This isn't completely unjustified. Riba, the architects' group, published some research in 2011 showing that the average three-bed home in the UK was 8 square metres smaller than the minimum recommended by London planning guidance. Now 8 square metres might not mean a lot to you, but it's roughly the size of a children's bedroom in these sorts of homes. So they found that three-bed homes were only the size of a two-bed home, squeezing people into what Riba called 'shameful shoebox homes'.

These pokey homes are often ridiculously expensive. The terms 'luxury apartments' and 'executive homes' just indicate an estate agent who lacked the imagination to sell a home on its merits, and who thought they could con buyers into thinking the shoebox was a mansion if they just stuck the word 'luxury' in front. But with prices so high, the terms are increasingly apt. The average price of a newly built home from the most recent official figures was £251,000 across the UK, and a ridiculous £511,000 in London.

With price tags like that, are local residents supposed to greet them as a solution to local housing problems? Even comfortable home-owners whose own homes are worth similar amounts are probably not particularly conscious of that fact, especially if they bought their home decades ago for a much more modest sum.

As prices have climbed, so have the incomes of the buyers. In pricey parts of the country, shock stories about foreign buyers and rich investors regularly make the headlines. In London – yes, the capital *again* – fully two-thirds of newly built homes are snapped up by investors. They might be a Chinese couple looking for a safe haven, or a Kent couple looking for a pension plan. It doesn't really matter where they are from; what matters is that they are buying up more and more homes.

It gets even worse when these new homes are proposed with very low levels of affordable housing. Every council sets its own requirements, but they are supposed to ensure that a decent number of the new homes are offered on social rents, or one of a growing list of convoluted schemes that are supposed to be more affordable than the open market.

Ideally, you'd work out how many people can't afford the open market, and set the requirement so that the equivalent number of homes are 'affordable'. But in very expensive areas this could mean more than eight in ten homes being affordable. In reality, it's often the reverse, with eight in ten being open market homes that only the very rich could afford to buy.

A third problem is where they are built. When a load of pokey executive homes are proposed for a field on the edge of town, locals may feel they have good, non-NIMBY reasons for objecting.

Greens want to protect productive farmland, wildlife-rich habitats and private gardens. We want to encourage more compact communities where cycling, walking and public transport are the norm, not cars. We want to stop sprawl. In theory we can achieve all of this and put homes in the best possible place. But again, annoying reality intrudes and makes life a bit more difficult. Brownfield sites are usually much more expensive to build on, and can often be rich with wildlife. Beautiful greenfield sites on the edges of towns and cities can be really near to a train station, making them in one respect a good choice for new homes. It all gets quite complicated.

Sham consultations

The underlying problem is that: of the way in which the standards for new homes and requirements for affordable housing are set, and which sites are earmarked for development, housing campaigners are involved in deciding none of these.

If you're the sort of person who can stomach spending a year or more reading thousands of pages of complicated planning policy, housing market assessments and the like, and then drafting lengthy consultation responses and attending dozens of council meetings to make your case, then you're well aware of how sites were chosen in your area. But most people aren't like this. They are just 'consulted' at the end of the process. If the word 'consultation' was given an honest definition in the English dictionary it would currently read: 'the act of seeking approval for a pre-determined option'.

All of this means that when new housing is proposed, it's opposed. That silver bullet, that most important solution, is deeply unpopular.

Making new homes popular

Let's tackle the affordability problem first. If a Green government increased the social housing budget, then new developments would be able to go ahead with much higher proportions of homes that local people can actually afford. Our policies to make the market more affordable, which I will come onto next, would also mean that the prices of these homes weren't quite so high. Within a generation, we could see new homes being built at prices that average house-holds could afford.

Greens also recognise that driving down standards is a self-defeating strategy. House builders have won over successive governments to this cause, arguing that if you make homes too expensive to build then fewer will go up. But if you make them so awful that nobody likes them, you're going to get justified opposition.

But getting higher standards isn't just a matter of improving planning policy, important though that is. We also have the problem that the planning system itself is pretty undemocratic, the preserve of wonks like me who know their LDFs from their SPGs.

I found inspiration for a much more radical change on continental Europe. Vauban is a large new neighbourhood built on an old French military base outside Freiburg in south-west Germany.

If this was in Britain, the site would have been sold to a really big developer, which would have developed plans for an uninspiring site full of tower blocks and empty green spaces, or mock-Tudor detached homes surrounding a golf course. But this site had been occupied for decades by hippies and anarchists, who eventually won the right to four of the twenty barracks. The council bought up the rest, and worked with an existing residents' group called Forum Vauban to collaborate on a 'masterplan' for the site. They worked out the car-free street layouts, the energy plans and other important features together.

The council then divided its land into lots of smaller plots and sold these to lots of small housing co-operatives and developers. Some were groups of self-builders, others commissioned builders to put up a block of flats for them. The whole site was a great big laboratory for different approaches to building, with some even refurbishing barracks.

If you're ever in that neck of the woods, you must visit the place. The result of this approach was a really wonderful new neighbourhood – designed around people instead of cars, with attractive homes built to high standards. This approach wasn't unique to Vauban. It's how lots of homes are built in countries like Germany, Austria, the Netherlands, even the USA. In the UK we call it 'custom build', and it would form the basis of a Green revolution in the planning system. Only the truly self-interested NIMBYs would object to new homes being built this way on a well-chosen site.

The problem of excess demand

Building homes in this 'custom-build' way might make people happier about the location and quality of the homes. But without other changes, they'd still be ridiculously expensive.

This is a bit of a chicken-and-egg problem. Building new homes is one way to reduce house prices. But new homes are opposed because they are too expensive. So we need something else to help break the cycle, to begin to stabilise and even bring prices down.

The reason homes are so expensive is that so many people want them. Obvious, right? But why do people want them, and why are they willing to pay so much for them? Most of us just want a home to live in, but a growing number of people also want a second home to holiday in, and perhaps a third home in the city for those evenings when they can't face the long commute back to their home counties house. As we get richer as a society – or at least some people do – the demand for housing increases. This can seriously distort local markets in seaside towns and city centres, which can then ripple out to the wider area. Usually these second-home owners earn a lot more than the local average, so can always bid higher than the nurse, baker or candlestick maker. This drives prices up.

More subtly, as we have become richer we have also been able to afford more space. The geographer Danny Dorling has pointed out that there are more bedrooms per person today than in the past, but they are very unequally distributed. The government has a bedroom standard, which says that having two bedrooms more than you need counts as 'under-occupation' and not having enough counts as 'over-crowding'. In the latest figures, about 3 per cent of households were overcrowded and 37 per cent were under-occupying. Generally, the richer homeowners are most likely to have lots of spare rooms, while low-income tenants are most likely to be overcrowded.

Now, personally, I think it's reasonable to have one or two spare rooms, especially if you want the family to stay for Christmas and somewhere to stash all those Green Party leaflets you need to deliver. There is an alternative called co-housing, where a local community shares some of that spare room in the form of extra rooms for family and friends to visit, community kitchens and so on. This can be an interesting and quite green way to make new neighbourhoods less wasteful, but it's hard to 'retrofit' it to existing terraced streets.

There is another really important reason why demand is so high

– property speculation. I mentioned earlier that a lot of homes these days seem to be bought up by investors, whether as a buy-to-let pension plan or a safe haven for overseas buyers. In London, as many as two-thirds of new homes are bought by investors! This adds yet more demand, and importantly it encourages people to pay above the odds in the belief that the value will only increase.

As interest rates have been kept very low, and deposit requirements on mortgages are cut back, it becomes cheap to borrow huge sums of money to pay for these second homes, spare bedrooms and speculative investments. All of these factors (and more I won't bore you with) add up to a problem called 'excess effective demand', which basically means that there are too many people willing and able to pay too much for housing.

Taxing demand away

As Greens, we're not afraid of using taxes to try and improve economic outcomes. We think the government should gradually change the tax system as one of a number of ways to reduce this demand. If we introduced some higher bands for council tax for the very pricey properties, we could make it more expensive to own them. We also want to charge premiums for second homes and empty homes to discourage those.

In the long term we would replace council tax completely with something called 'land value tax', which would charge you in proportion to the value of the land under your home. This has some other nice benefits like incentivising compact towns and cities, but the main point here is that it could be used to tax away the unearned wealth that people get by speculating on property.

Bringing housing policy back to homes

If I were to sum up the Green approach to housing, it would be quite simple: houses aren't assets to speculate on, they aren't boxes that people will enjoy no matter how unattractive, they aren't abstract units to demolish without regard to the people who live in them, and they shouldn't be built without regard to other species who live here too. We want to guarantee everybody their right to a secure, affordable and comfortable home, and in a way that leaves space for wildlife.

We undoubtedly have a grave housing crisis, but it isn't going to end if we just intone 'build more houses'.

Tom Chance is an amateur cartographer, cyclist and green activist. In his day job he supports Green Party politicians in the London Assembly on housing, planning and economic policy. @tom_chance

Chapter 11

Transport

CAROLINE RUSSELL

I'm an elected councillor in Islington and a long-term transport campaigner. I was prompted to start campaigning twenty-two years ago when I first had children and started to see streets from the perspective of someone encumbered by a pram. It opened my eyes to the experience of older people and those with disabilities, gave me a taste for local politics and showed me the power of building coalitions of support as a way to bring about change in my local area by improving crossings, reducing lorry danger and controlling vehicle speeds. By the time I realised I wanted to stand for election, the only political party that had the right policies on local transport was the Green Party, so I signed up and have never looked back.

I shall introduce our transport policy and outline the problems we hope to solve along with some practical solutions. First, an overview.

Prioritising other forms of transport

Our national, local and personal transport choices have implications for our quality of life, the national economy, local economies, our health and the environment. So transport policy is not just about transport. We would prioritise some forms of transport over others. On a spectrum: walk; cycle; take the bus or train; freight, motorcycle;

car; plane – our policies are designed to make it easier to do things at the 'walking' end of the spectrum, and less convenient/more expensive to do things at the 'flying' end. This will encourage changes in transport choices, benefiting health, the environment, the economy and (ultimately) the climate.

Very broadly and keeping it simple this would involve:

- Prioritising walking and cycling, making them safe, convenient and pleasant choices for local journeys.
- Taking a road danger reduction approach. Slowing vehicle speeds to 20 mph on all residential streets and on main roads where people live, work and shop, making them more 'liveable' and safer.
- Reintroducing proper regulation of buses, with local authorities having responsibility to ensure a reliable and convenient public service along with integrated ticketing like the Oyster card in London.
- Using the planning system to encourage mixed-use developments where shops, housing and business are closely co-located, creating active communities and reducing commuting. We would also ensure new developments are well served by public transport, walking and cycling routes.
- Taking the railways back into public ownership: rail is an essential public service and should be run for public benefit, not private gain. The East Coast Mainline has been in public ownership since 2009, and returned £200 million to the taxpayer this year: the government's desire to re-privatise it is purely ideological.
- Introducing taxation on aviation to reflect its full environmental costs (the 'polluter pays' principle). Failing to tax aviation fuel and choosing not to levy VAT on tickets and aircraft amounts to a £10 billion annual subsidy in the UK alone. We would oppose the expansion of UK airports.

You'll note there is no mention of the government's recently announced road expansion programme on the list. Greens oppose the building of new roads on the basis that the money would be far better invested in local rail and bus services and in providing routes to enable local trips on foot and by bike. If you build more roads you get more traffic and congestion, air pollution and road danger. New roads fill up fast and quickly become clogged with traffic, blighting the lives of travellers and residents of the communities severed by multi-lane highways. Building more roads is the wrong solution, and let me say why.

Just five years ago people were making the case for active travel and public transport on the basis of their potential to reduce carbon emissions along with an urgent call to reduce road death and injury. Today, while carbon reduction is still crucial, people are presenting the case for changes to transport planning in terms of supporting local economic activity, addressing health inequality and improving our quality of life. Further, campaigners are shifting the debate so that while road death reduction is still an absolute priority, the case is being framed around promoting more liveable villages, towns and cities, with cleaner air and improved public health.

Living in London, I've seen the current Mayor galvanising campaigners to articulate a clear vision for a different way to plan transport in our city. Those of us concerned about the lot of pedestrians were concerned that one of Boris Johnson's first actions on becoming Mayor was to cancel the Year of Walking. This was followed by his promoting a programme of smoothing traffic flow, which motivated an explosion of focused and effective campaigning, with high-profile stunts, vigils and an online blossoming of ideas and debate amongst campaigners, journalists, bloggers and politicians. This has been both desperately sad, as more and more people have lost their lives on the road, and also extraordinarily inspiring, as we have seen so many people add their thoughtful contributions to a debate about how transport can do more for our capital city.

The rate of death and injury that is tolerated on our road system has been designed out on the railways. There is a stark asymmetry of risk on our roads where the most vulnerable – on foot, on bikes and even on horses – are disproportionately killed and injured. The media frequently blames traffic victims implicitly by mentioning they were wearing dark clothes, had consumed alcohol or had no helmet. While it may make sense to wear something reflective at night and to have working lights if riding a bike, we need to ensure that people in cars, vans, lorries and buses are driving carefully and considerately and that they anticipate people crossing the road with impaired judgement after pub closing time. The price of a slight mistake by a driver, a pedestrian or a cyclist is too often the death or serious injury of someone on foot or on a bike. If we accept that price, we give our roads, all that public space, exclusively to those travelling in motorised vehicles, which is clearly not right.

Liveable cities

All the NGOs will tell you we need a shift in the way our cities and our transport system are run:

- Campaign for Better Transport will tell you: build roads and you get traffic (congestion, pollution, danger) – so don't.
- Living Streets will make a strong case for more time to cross the road, particularly for older people and children.
- Transport for All will tell you we need inclusive streets, with accessible public transport and pavements and step-free tube access.
- Roadpeace call for traffic justice, road danger reduction and more support for the families of road traffic victims.
- 20's Plenty For Us have been raising awareness of car dependency while focused on one issue – speed reduction. This has actually brought to the fore the wider impact of car culture on our daily lives.

- London Cycling Campaign have been game changing with their call for 'Space for Cycling', Dutch design standards and making space for people.

The debate has been exhilarating and has included countless contributions from bloggers, NGOs and people who care. The debate has focused on liveable cities, towns and villages and an understanding that it is not just about cycling: rather, it is about living well with fewer cars. When Jan Gehl, Danish architect and urban design consultant, came to speak in Hackney earlier this year, the Hackney Empire was sold out; so many people wanted to hear his vision for liveable cities, where cars are guests. His claim that 'if you build space for people, you get people' went down a storm.

Part of the rapidly shifting picture has been air pollution. The awareness of the impact of diesel particulates on our health is growing, in no small part due to campaigns such as the Clean Air London campaign, where Simon Birkett has built cross-party support for measures to reduce our exposure to air pollution.

The World Health Organization recently designated diesel particulate pollution as carcinogenic. This is a game changer, or at least it should be. Studies of summer 2014 showed exposure levels inside cars and buses were higher than for people walking and cycling. I suspect we will look back at the diesel particulate pollution with horror, rather as we view poisoning ourselves with leaded petrol in the past. Clearly, we have to urgently reduce car use and rid our towns and cities of diesel vehicles. This requires Ultra Low Emission Zones and viable convenient alternatives to car use to be made available both in our cities and in rural areas. The car market has been ignoring the growing body of evidence to show that diesel vehicles are utterly unsuitable for use in towns and cities and it will take brave political action to make diesel pollution a thing of the past.

There are some current opportunities that offer a real route to change things and help to underpin a Green transport vision:

Public health and local authorities

Public health being devolved to local authorities lends an extraordinary opportunity to shape a vision for more integrated transport planning linked to public health outcomes. In my borough, Islington, we see one in ten children obese as they enter reception and a quarter overweight. By Year 6, one in five are obese and a third are overweight. Public health professionals speak about physical activity as almost a magic bullet that tackles a range of health issues – obesity, type 2 diabetes, lung and heart health problems and even social isolation in older people. By making it easy to build walking and cycling into daily trips, we can help people stay well and improve population-wide public health outcomes.

There is a tension where political leadership is required. Parking provision brings in revenue to cash-strapped councils but also brings in more vehicle trips along with more road danger, pollution and congestion. In London, vehicle ownership is falling yet the removal of a single car-parking space is still a political hot potato. This has to change.

The local authorities with politicians demonstrating political vision to integrate public health thinking and active travel into their transport departments will reap the benefits of more liveable, people-friendly streets and a more active population with potential for a future reduction in the currently escalating budgets for adult social care.

Active Travel Act

In Wales they have gone a step further and legislated for active travel. The Active Travel Act for Wales builds in physical activity by creating and updating active travel networks and bringing active travel considerations into planning decisions.

Many car trips are made because people feel they have no alternative. Rural roads are frightening to cycle on and there are few public transport options. Public transport needs to be affordable and regular and should connect places where people want to go. New housing shouldn't get permission unless there is access to public transport and good routes for walking and cycling. Those meandering estate roads designed for cars, with no direct walking route to get anywhere, should be outlawed. The implementation of the Act will be the proof of the pudding but, as an expression of a political vision for transport, it is inspiring and most definitely Green.

Cycling Delivery Plan

The government has announced a Cycling Delivery Plan. It is good to know that it exists and it's very good to see that walking is included, but it really doesn't go far enough. They are just proposing to double funding by 2021 to £10 per head per annum, which is really not ambitious enough and amounts to a few hundred million pounds – a mere drop in the ocean compared to the billions being spent on new roads.

If we achieve our marvellous networks of safe and convenient walking and cycling routes, they need to connect with places people want to go and with integrated, affordable and efficient public transport systems that let people travel when and where they need to travel.

Re-regulation of buses

London has had an integrated Oyster ticketing system for several years, which has helped make public transport convenient and user-friendly. Recently, Newcastle has taken steps towards re-regulation of their buses. In autumn 2014, the North East Combined Authority voted to refer the Quality Contract Scheme for Tyne and Wear buses to the next stage. The councillors rejected both the bus operators' proposed Voluntary Partnership Agreement and the 'do minimum' option that would have seen further decline and cuts in bus services. By doing this, they are allowing for a vision of an affordable and user-friendly alternative to the private car.

Transport vision

The opportunities are clear. We could have massive improvements in public health, along with savings in NHS bills, and all it needs is for us to reduce our dependence on private motor vehicles and develop networks – with integration both for local walking and cycling trips but also for buses, tubes and trains for longer journeys. It should be easy. But it is not so easy in practice and I think the reason the current Mayor of London has struggled to get his vision to work is that his vision has not embraced the questions about the suitability of motor cars as a city transport mode that are being asked by public health officials, campaigners and urban designers.

I represented Living Streets on Transport for London's Junction Review, looking at the most dangerous junctions. The tension between the Mayor's desire to smooth vehicle flow and the need to create space for cycling and walking provided a major topic of debate across the table. It felt as if officers were attempting to deliver an almost impossible vision that had to both prioritise vehicle flow and create space and time for active travel modes. However, it does seem that the groundswell of campaigning voices is being heard. More and more junctions are coming through where both time and space are being given to cycling and walking.

For me, it clarifies the importance of being very clear about political objectives. What is the priority for delivery? Politicians need to provide leadership and clear vision in order that decisions are taken and measures implemented. As a Green, the vision is about addressing public health, reducing health inequality, ensuring road justice and making streets, villages, towns and cities that are great places to be. That means cleaning up the air with Ultra Low emission zones and removing diesel from our cities; reducing road danger, and particularly danger from lorries, with slower speeds; prioritising walking, cycling and public transport; and reducing the need and convenience of choosing to travel by car.

I spent an afternoon recently in a classroom at a school in my ward talking with six- and seven-year-olds about streets. Leaving aside the occasional snake, frog and an aeroplane, they were very articulate in their vision of good streets: it included planting, seating, lots of crossings, shops, places to visit, public transport, bikes and bike parking. They were very grumpy about lorries and buses blocking crossings when the green man was showing. It was almost as if they had intuited Jan Gehl and his inspirational vision for liveable cities where cars are mere guests. If children can see so clearly how to get it right, we adults should be able to make it happen.

Caroline Russell is Green councillor for Highbury East and parliamentary candidate for Islington North. She is the party's national spokesperson on local transport. @highburyonfoot

Chapter 12

Environment

SHASHA KHAN

I shall use my experience of campaigning against an incinerator proposal as a case study that affects both environment and human health. I also want to detail the lack of principle of the other parties on that issue and explain what I mean by environment. First, some preliminaries.

Harms of incineration

Incinerators release a variety of chemicals and fine particles. The chemicals include lead, cadmium and mercury, which are not destroyed by incineration, and dioxins, which, like fine particles, are created in the burning process.

The metals are poisonous. Dioxins are extremely toxic. According to the World Health Organization, they 'can cause reproductive and developmental problems, damage the immune system, interfere with hormones and also cause cancer'. We would therefore expect more illness near to incinerators and that's what we find. For instance:

- Between 1974 and 1987, cancer was twice as common in children living near UK incinerators as elsewhere.

- An Italian study in 1996 found lung cancer deaths near to an incinerator to be nearly seven times higher than elsewhere.

So we should not build more incinerators. There are other reasons, too. The government of the day needs to enforce the waste hierarchy – and working down the inverse pyramid, the maximum level of waste needs to be treated at each stage to leave only waste which can't be reused, recycled or composted to be disposed of using residual technology. Looming EU fines for sending waste to landfill are a driver for this change and councils are incentivised to opt for incineration, even though the alternatives are cheaper, more sustainable and create jobs.

Waste strategy

Greens see waste as a resource. Waste has a value and that value is lost forever when the waste it is buried in a landfill or burnt in an incinerator. Yes, in some cases energy can be used from burning waste but it is not an efficient solution. The most sustainable solution is a zero-waste strategy, and communities in Europe that adopt this solution are achieving 85 per cent recycling rates.

A zero-waste strategy includes but goes well beyond recycling. It prefers reducing stuff to reusing it and reusing stuff to recycling. It requires co-operation between industry, government and citizens to:

- Buy less but better stuff.
- Design processes so as not to produce waste.
- Design products to support repair, reuse of components and recycling.
- Reuse products by passing them to additional users.
- Separate out stuff than can be recycled and pass it to appropriate processors.
- Compost organic waste.

Campaign against incinerator

In spring 2013, I was sitting opposite a Labour councillor in the London borough of Croydon, flanked by two fellow 'Stop the Incinerator' campaigners. We were desperate men, but for very different reasons. Just a week earlier, Sutton council's planning committee had approved a 302,000-tonne commercial and domestic waste incinerator, to be constructed about half a mile from where we were meeting. The Labour Party in Croydon had been campaigning against the incinerator. A few Labour activists and councillors had come to a film screening of *Trashed* that I and fellow campaigners had put on which exposed the health risks from modern waste incinerators.

After two terms sitting on the opposition benches, Labour were determined to win back control of Croydon Council. The Conservatives controlled the council with thirty-seven seats to Labour's thirty-three. Waddon, the most marginal seat in the borough, happened to be on the border of Sutton and Croydon. For Labour, the incinerator issue had to stay alive. While it could be argued that it hadn't been the be-all and end-all of issues on the doorstep in Waddon, it was certainly good ammunition to throw at the Conservatives.

We were told that if we campaigners could stall the construction of the incinerator by launching a legal challenge, then, if Labour won control of the council, it would pull out of the South London Waste Partnership (SLWP) made up of the councils of Croydon, Sutton, Merton and Kingston. The SLWP had six months earlier signed a 25-year waste contract, part of a concurrent procurement process, with waste company Viridor as a forerunner to acquiring planning consent to construct the incinerator.

Before this, those of us involved in the campaign had already completed the preliminaries with regard to a legal challenge. We had met with our London-based solicitors. The problem was that the projected costs were prohibitive.

The nonsensical thing about the meeting with Croydon Labour is that if Labour, at that point in time, controlled the council then our allies would have been the Conservative Party. In fact, this environmental issue had exposed the lack of principle amongst Labour, Conservatives and the Lib Dems to a level that was farcical. Here's why.

Back in 2003, four south London boroughs (Croydon, Sutton, Kingston and Merton) pooled their collective waste in order to offer economies of scale to a prospective waste contractor. Nine years later, this inter-authority partnership, called the South London Waste Partnership (SLWP) signed a contract with the waste company Viridor. The signatory to the SLWP/Viridor contract in Croydon was the Conservative Party. The opposition party in Croydon, Labour, opposed the incinerator. In neighbouring Merton, the Labour Party had signed the contract and the Conservatives and Lib Dems had opposed it. In Kingston, the Lib Dems were in favour and had signed the contract and the Conservatives offered token resistance there. When I tell people this, they nearly always laugh. Then, as this reality hits home, they usually become irritated or angry before asking despairingly, 'What can you do?' I say you can start by voting Green.

The incinerator issue had exposed the complete lack of principle with regard to the environment for all three parties. When speaking at the planning meeting at Lib Dem-controlled Sutton Council, which subsequently approved the incinerator, I started off my speech by saying, 'If the Liberal Democrats on this council were in opposition, their colleagues would be sitting in this chair, their friends and family would be in the public gallery, struggling to comprehend how the council can take such an immoral decision.'

Across the country, eighty different campaign groups, which include combinations of the three main parties and Greens, are fighting different combinations of the three main parties to stop their respective incinerator. How can this be?

What is undoubtedly missing is a core principle to guide Labour, the Lib Dems and the Conservatives. The first and third of the ten principles which make up the Green Party's Core Values – specifically, on environmental justice and sustainability – guide and motivate Greens on this issue. There can be fewer greater injustices than poisoning people!

The Stop the Incinerator campaign decided that I should become claimant for the legal challenge. I ended up challenging Sutton Council in the High Court through a judicial review. I recall that friends from all over the world were interested in what I had started on social media and were sharing our crowdfunding site. One friend in Texas messaged his friends on Facebook to please support me because 'he's protecting the environment'. It was interesting to see how he had synthesised the Facebook posts and viewed the issue as environmental. However, I've never been keen for this to be pigeonholed as an environmental issue. For me it was, first and foremost, a health issue. Burning rubbish in modern incinerators doesn't stop emissions. As a fellow campaigner in the Merton Conservative Party maintained, if it has a chimney it has emissions. This incinerator will have two chimneys reaching up 95 metres into the sky.

Stopping the incinerator could be seen as an environmental/ecological issue if you consider that recyclables will be burnt. It could be also seen as a financial issue, a projected pressure on the health service over the next twenty-five years, particularly when the Mayor of London says that one in twelve deaths in London are attributable to poor air quality. However, councils are not really considering social and environmental costs when taking decisions. Cash-strapped councils across the country are persuaded to support the technology proposed and opted for by the winning waste contractor. This is principally down to savings from the projected landfill tax bill. Equally, waste contractors are not considering social and environmental costs because these don't affect their calculations when projecting the bottom line.

Dictionary.com defines 'environment' as 1. *The aggregate of surrounding things, conditions or influences.* 2. *Ecology. The air, water, minerals, organisms and all other external factors surrounding and affecting a given organism at any time.* The second definition is arguably the most commonly accepted understanding of the word environment in this context. The third listed result fascinates me greatly: *The social and cultural forces that shape the life of a person, or a population.*

Whatever the precise definition, the environment ought to be the concern that should top every pollster's issue of the day. However, this is not apparent. An IPSOS Mori poll in September 2014 asked, '*What do you see as the most/other important issues facing Britain today?*' Environment did not appear in the top ten mentions, yet issues such as poverty, which did appear, are still relevant here.

The wards directly downwind from the proposed incinerator are associated with higher levels of poverty than others in the borough. There are fewer university-educated professionals living here. Croydon's Broad Green ward, alongside Waddon, will experience the highest levels of pollution from the incinerator. Broad Green ward experienced the brunt of the economic riots that engulfed this country in the summer of 2011. Shops were torched and razed to the ground there.

Friends of the Earth conducted a study which showed that 50 per cent of all the incinerators are in 10 per cent of the poorest wards in the country. This is unsurprising because poorer wards simply don't have the technical and financial expertise to stop incinerators, mainly because the vast majority of people living in these wards are more concerned with day-to-day issues like paying the rent or mortgage, getting food on the table and buying school uniforms for their children. It is the inequality ingrained in our society that ensures that poorer communities will be subject to social injustices like the use of these giant incinerators. This in turn means that their homes become less comparatively valuable. Indeed, of the £25,000 raised thus far to pay for legal bills for the judicial review, very little has come from wards immediately downwind.

A study in *The Guardian* revealed that in terms of job creation, incinerators were a poor option. Including apprenticeships, the number of employees working at the planned incinerator is forty. The *Guardian* report indicated that 400 jobs could be created if the recyclables, instead of being burnt, were sorted in a job-rich reuse and recycle facility. San Francisco shows the way globally with 80 per cent recycling.

Air pollution is a killer. The site of the planned incinerator actually falls within an air quality management area – yet such is the pathetic regulation regarding this type of pollution that road widening and other nonsensical solutions are deemed adequate mitigation. It seems that existing air pollution somehow makes new air pollution acceptable. Already, 4,000 deaths are attributable to poor air quality in London per year, which obviously applies more pressure on our creaking NHS.

This incinerator does nothing for race relations either. I was once approached by a Labour member who was disillusioned by the prospect of the planned incinerator belching out toxic emissions in an area where ethnic minorities predominately lived.

As said, the riots in Croydon were felt mostly in Broad Green ward. Local people without a stake in society turned on the community they lived in. I was asked to give a presentation about the incinerator to the Broad Green Business Forum. Apart from the chair, who was wheelchair bound, all the business owners in the room were Asian Indian. Many were still rebuilding their businesses. This is a vulnerable community already feeling undervalued, and telling them about the planned incinerator further affirmed their opinions.

In May 2014, the Labour Party did win control of Croydon council, with a majority. Croydon have not pulled out of the South London Waste Partnership because the cost of withdrawing from their contractual obligations would allegedly cost 'tens of millions'. Inside Croydon, a local news site reminded us of Labour's political posturing:

> Croydon's Conservative council has ignored the views of local people
> by ... supporting an incinerator at Beddington Lane. Labour has always

opposed this; a truly green council would never support the building of
an incinerator that will be a potential health risk on its border, particularly one so close to residential areas.

Environment as more than rolling fields

I hope to have shown that the environment is highly relevant to the
lives of people. Yet in the minds of the population, the visual image
of the environment is often that of the countryside. As if to confirm
my thoughts, on the night of writing this section, the BBC showed
images of rolling fields to depict the environment when explaining
the harm that fracking can do. In view of the above, surely a more
powerful and equally accurate depiction would be to use footage of
people struggling to survive and being displaced due to desertifica-
tion as a result of an increase in global temperatures. I have long
felt that names given to issues have an impact on their importance
within the psyche of the people. Climate change is a good example.
It really doesn't suggest anything harmful. The fact that millions
of people will be displaced leading to starvation, or that extreme
weather conditions will be experienced, indicates that people do
and will die because of climate change. So surely 'climate death' is a
more appropriate term?

Similarly, one of the obstacles to the growth of the Green Party
is its name. Green suggests that we are only interested in the environment. In 2008, I canvassed a house in Bensham Manor ward in
Croydon. The householder was an Asian gentleman who was engaging, I think partly because he was intrigued to see an Asian candidate
representing the Green Party and not Labour. 'You see, the problem
with the Green Party is that it is only concerned with the environment.' I assume when he saw my Green Party rosette when he opened
the door, the temporal lobe in his brain triggered images of rolling fields. I replied spontaneously with, 'I actually joined the Green
Party because of the war in Iraq.' This had become my stock reply if

someone pointed out the single-issue misconception. What I should have replied was, 'I am concerned about the social and cultural forces that shape the life of a person or a population, aren't you?'

Bensham Manor is, relatively speaking, a non-affluent ward with a big ethnic minority population. Many don't speak English as a first language. I recall canvassing a house in the ward where I was greeted with enthusiasm by a lady with a strong African accent who said, 'The environment is important because it is everywhere.' Her understanding of the environment was far greater than the stock image of rolling fields. She recognised the interconnectedness of all things. Short-term decision-making over issues such as waste management leads to poor air quality, which affects the health of a community, resulting in greater pressure on the health service.

One of the former registered descriptions of the Green Party which could have been used by the candidate on the ballot paper used to be: *Green Party – The Party for the Environment*. Could this be stating the obvious? Today's list no longer carries this moniker. Instead we have *Green Party – Say No To Racism* and *Green Party – Stop Fracking Now*.

Unarguably, the Green Party is associated with the environment owing to its name and origins. I imagine that most people are concerned about the environment if they understand that to mean *the social and cultural forces that shape the life of a person or a population* or *the aggregate of surrounding things, conditions or influences*. One could conclude that the population is more concerned about the environment but they may not know it because maybe the media prefers to report on more in-your-face issues that are triggered by natural human fear, such as immigration.

My political colleague Brendan Walsh once tweeted, 'You're all Green, you just don't know it yet.' This was a reaction to the results from completed surveys on the Vote for Policies website. Nearly half a million surveys have been completed by people comparing policies from six political parties on a range of key issues. The result thus far shows that Greens are topping the polls with 26 per cent.

On the specific issue of the environment, Greens top the poll with 30 per cent.

So, why vote Green? I would say that the environment is, for Greens, by virtue of the origins of the party and our core values, our natural territory. Other parties tend to be tokenistic and lacking in consistency and principle on this issue. However, the environment is so much more than what the media conveys through its rolling hills imagery. In truth, it is all of the influences and external factors, along with the social and cultural forces, that affect our quality of life. What's more, the average voter is actually more concerned about the environment than they realise. They just don't know it yet.

Shasha Khan lives in Selhurst, Croydon with his wife and daughter. He is Green Party parliamentary candidate for Croydon North and is currently campaigning to stop the south London incinerator. @GreenKnight2010

Chapter 13

International Affairs

TONY CLARKE

Internationalism

The Green Party has always taken a broad, internationalist view on what is needed to change our world for the better. We have always been global in our thinking and we offer a more radical programme for world change than any other UK political party. On international affairs our vision is so different that for many new members it forms the prime reason for joining the party. Tackling climate change and fighting for social justice have their roots within local communities, but both can only truly be achieved through international cooperation and action.

By comparison, the protectionist bleatings of successive Foreign Secretaries and their official opposition counterparts in Parliament and on our TV screens can often sound hollow and condescending. The unhealthy and at times deceitful relationship that currently exists between state and subject can perhaps best be analogised through the use of a short comic interlude. In series one of the TV comedy *The League of Gentlemen*, set in a fictional Pennines village, local shopkeeper Tubbs Tattysrup is to be seen crying while reading a road map. When her husband Edward enters the room she looks up at him tearfully and exclaims aloud, 'You lied to me Edward, there *IS* a Swansea, and other places too!' He replies, 'Yes, I kept them from you Tubbs! To keep you pure and clean and *local*!'

Edward's presumed comfort in shaping Tubbs's view of the outside world through the use of enforced ignorance and deception is just a humorous parody of life in an excluded remote community. But similar methods being deployed by ministers and senior politicians have a more serious and more dangerous impact. Their manipulative verbal downpours often shower down on to a British public, sometimes leading us to wrongfully support wars or to mistreat our international neighbours. Whether speaking in the Commons or being interviewed by the media, our senior politicians are at times simply trying to defend Britain's unjustified aggressions against other nation states, or they are cheerleaders for attempts to colour public opinion against those other countries they wish us to hold in contempt. This rhetoric is not only damaging to the UK's standing abroad but can lead to massive injustices, poverty and, far too frequently, the loss of life in other countries.

The continued use of deceit and jingoism by some UK politicians, and also by a large proportion of our national media, is now thankfully meeting with opposition. Via the internet, we hear contrasting opinions and are provided with an alternative view to that handed down to us by the establishment. Through the use of social media and local blogs, ordinary people are speaking out and, as a result, those less gullible are starting to think and speak out for themselves.

For the Green Party this is a welcome phenomenon which assists us in promoting our views and ideas as to how we can change Britain for the common good and change the way our Parliament works. We strive for a future in which the UK is seen as a promoter and defender, not an enemy, of international justice and world peace.

Our philosophical basis underpins everything we do and is a very good place to start any examination of policy. We begin recording these underlying principles by stating that 'a world based on cooperation and democracy would prioritise the many, not the few, and would not risk the planet's future with environmental destruction and unsustainable consumption'.

Our values are internationalist at their very roots. We value and practise individual and collective self-expression and self-determination. Each and every policy intervention and statement will start from a principled examination of what people on the ground, in the communities and countries affected by world events, really want for themselves.

It is certainly not for any one party or indeed government to determine the futures of people not under their jurisdiction, and it should also be the collective role of governments to only intervene to enable and protect that self-determination when it is threatened by corruption of power or armed force. So how we react to the problems of the world is of primary importance.

In recent times, it feels as if the world is in a state of perpetual war. Conflict follows on from conflict; democratic unrest and even peaceful revolution are too often replaced by military dictatorship or unsustainable governance.

International arms sales are soaring. New modern weaponry in many cases is now computerised, able to wreak ever growing pain to civilian populations, and yet the reasons for conflict, war and displacement of people remain the same today as they have ever been – the brutal pursuit of power, land and money. How should we respond politically to this growing tyranny?

Many political parties both within the UK and in the wider world have no clear foundation or philosophical basis for their responses to either international conflict or disasters and, as a consequence, muddle along with confused and ever changing policies and reactionary attitudes which fail to deal with the problems of our world.

So-called special relationships, historical hangovers or even personal self-interest drive governmental international policy far more than is decent or credible. The people of the UK have been accustomed to taking their lead, forming their opinion of the outside world based not on facts but on prejudice; on perceived, rather than real, risk, and also on the say-so of our insincere senior politicians and the media outlets that support them.

But the world is becoming smaller by the day, and information often accessed on the internet cannot be so easily censored and controlled. Increasingly, people are starting to question their masters and openly challenge the decisions they try to take on our behalf.

The horrific recent wars in Afghanistan and Iraq perpetrated by Western coalition partners indifferent to the protests from many within their respective nations are now often referred to as 'game changers' for future international interventions and actions. In the Green Party we are encouraged to see that people themselves are beginning to form their own opinions on international affairs and we are confident that the more they do so, the more they will look to politically radical movements like us for solutions.

Cooperation and globalisation

The Green Party is also a party of peace and, while we would always prefer to use diplomacy to resolve international conflict before considering any agreed international military intervention, we are also very aware of the responsibility of the world to act as a protector of human rights and life, and as a reliever of suffering. While we wish to see NATO disbanded, we do aspire to a strengthening of the United Nations and its mandate and we acknowledge the need to advance continental agreements and actions through organisations such as the Organisation for Security and Cooperation in Europe (OSCE).

We believe the interests of the world are further advanced and enhanced by the development of stronger roles for joined-up decision-making to resolve international conflict and end the oppression of world communities and peoples.

Taking on the multinational corporations and their stranglehold on those who govern us is perhaps the greatest and most difficult challenge we face. The greed of global banking institutions has brought the old world order and our economy to its knees, and in doing so helped to unmask the real villain of the piece, but the villain will still need to be apprehended and then brought to justice if we are to ever replace a consumer-driven society with one that places more importance on matters of global sustainability and collective, not individual need.

Global and international structures and institutions should always be based on the principle of co-operation. Power should mostly remain at the local, community level with sustainable, localised economies under democratic control. This power should only be ceded upwards when absolutely necessary.

Such massive changes to not only our nation's governance but also to our world economy cannot be achieved in the short-term, immediate future. Such a transition will take a long time; therefore we will first have to ensure that existing centralised structures of governance, such as the EU, are decentralised to appropriate and effective levels, depending on the issue in hand. International structures and institutions need to be transformed from being nationally based to being based on confederations of (sub-national) regions or localities. When the present government talk of EU reform, they talk of controls on the freedom of movement or for tax breaks for big business, whereas a Green government would reform the EU in the people's favour not for the benefit of the few.

In similar fashion, we need to encourage all national governments to decentralise their powers and functions, increase real democracy internally and increase the localisation of production and consumption.

But we will still need to trade, albeit more locally. Therefore we also need to secure a general agreement on sustainable trade, under which fair trade applies. This would become a prerequisite for international trade and the local supply of goods. These agreements should replace the General Agreement on Tariffs and Trade (GATT), a World

Localisation Organisation should replace the World Trade Organization (WTO) and business-friendly stitch-up agreements like TTIP (Transatlantic Trade & Investment Partnership) should be scrapped. A new global agreement on investment and ownership should be agreed to enshrine the right of local government to enact legislation to stabilise and protect the local economy, such as 'site here to sell here' rules.

So that's the vision, those are the principles. But how do they then translate into policy and action? And how is Britain's attitude to war changing as an ever more informed public engage in the debate on Britain's future role in an ever troubled world? Let us take the West's interventions in the Arab and Muslim world and in the Middle East as an example.

Weapons of mass distraction

There is a widely held view, prominent within the British media, that Labour backbench rebellion against the Iraq War in 2004 was predominantly based on rejection at the time of the 'dodgy dossier', warning of Iraq's stocks of chemical and possible nuclear weaponry. Parliament gave voice to this red herring through speeches in the chamber on the past and future roles of weapons inspectors and the need for greater clarity on shared intelligence on chemical and nuclear weapons.

Yet for me, as one of many anti-war Labour MPs at the time, weapons of mass destruction were always far less concerning than the weapons of mass distraction being employed by Bush and Blair to try to excuse their warmongering and their ulterior motives. Then, I was also a member of the Labour friends of the Middle East and our own discussions over what was occurring were always far more expansive, and our concerns far more plural. Those concerns were, as they always had been, about the continued fragility of the Middle East states and the concern that constant interference by the West in the affairs of these states could only ever lead to further unrest.

These states were created on borders drawn up and imposed by 'outsiders' undermining local self-determination and preventing any internal Arab solution being found. So we should be clear on the real cause of the current bloodletting in Iraq and Syria: let us place the blame squarely where it should rest. The blood indelibly stains the hands of both Tony Blair and George W. Bush.

I recall in 2004 being interviewed under caution by Special Branch officers after a transcript of a meeting between the President and Prime Minister came into my possession via my political assistant. The document, you may recall, was given back to No. 10, as its disclosure at that time, in my view, would have placed British troops engaged in the 'theatre of war' in danger. The two spooks interviewing me were keen to ask questions on my view of President Bush, mostly because I had already admitted discussing the document with colleagues from the Democrat Party in the States. I said that in my view President Bush was the most dangerous man on the planet and that despite his own well-documented claims, the true axis of evil existed far closer to his home than he had previously suggested and was in fact resident within the White House. The two officers were aghast: how could a member of the UK Parliament hold such 'extremist' views? Well, perhaps if they are reading this today they will understand far better the basis for my concerns.

As ISIS/ISIL/Daish (Islamic State of Iraq and the Levant) continues its offence against ill-prepared Iraqi troops and Syrian factions to build a Sunni-based Islamic State which recognises no borders, the true cost of the West's illegal occupation of Iraq becomes ever more apparent. Do we never learn?

Failed interventions

The truth is really very simple: any military occupation of any country will simply act as a recruitment agent for the forces rallied against you, and any puppet regime placed in power by an evacuating army will always fall over simply by being labelled from the start by local communities as contaminated goods.

Blair, of course, thinks very differently. He dismisses the claims of those of us who believe his war on terror simply made a bad situation a critical one. He says about the current crisis in Iraq that 'we have to liberate ourselves from the notion that we have caused this', and there he goes again, trying to 'liberate' notions this time instead of nations! Which I guess is an improvement, but it doesn't hold true.

Despite the loss of well over one million troops, insurgents and civilians in Iraq and Afghanistan since Bush and Blair's wars began, my former party leader still wants us to hold onto the premise that without his involvement it could all have been worse! Open civil war; the use of chemical weapons by all sides; rape used as a war weapon; hundreds of thousands of children dead and dying through hunger and disease; neighbours killing neighbours; ancient cities flattened; villages wiped out and the numbers of fundamental extremists increased tenfold – and he suggests it could have been worse! It just doesn't ring true.

What is true, of course, is that the enforced borders and invented nation states such as those of Iraq, established by the British Empire in 1921, and of Syria, a 1922 creation of French/British making which also formed the lands of Lebanon and British-controlled Palestine, are going to be continuously challenged and fought over by local tribes and faith-based militants.

This will continue until such a time that the Middle East is shaped in a form acceptable to those living in the Middle East rather than that only acceptable to Western governments still intent on manipulating their own imposed regimes for their own ends.

It is also worth remembering when trying to work out what has gone wrong in Syria that, before 1945, the French Mandate created different states in Aleppo, Damascus, Alexandretta, Apatite, Greater Lebanon and Jabal Al Druze, and that borders in Mesopotamia were also redrawn, ignoring the views of those in Kurdistan who were to be denied autonomy for decades to come. And yet now we try to preach to the dispossessed the language of unity!

The answer to the current crisis in the Middle East is not to be found looking down the barrel of guns, whether those in the hands of Western soldiers or those sold or gifted to Al Qaeda by Western governments. It is to be found internally through negotiation (enforced, if necessary, with Arab peacekeeping forces on the ground) and through the continued involvement of the Arab League Council. My current belief, uncomfortable as it may seem both to the West and to those of us who seek co-existence and secular nations, is that the days of Iraq as a nation state could now be numbered and that will inevitably leave us with separate Sunni, Shia and Kurdish states.

At the moment, the need to stop the bloodshed is, of course, far greater than any desire for perfect multifaceted Muslim nations, but if there is a hope of fixing Iraq's damaged democracy and creating an Iraq and a Syria where Kurds, Shia and Sunni Muslims and Christians can live in peace together then the UK and the US need to learn the lessons of the past: keep our distance.

All humans equal value

Israel–Palestine, Syria–Iraq, Afghanistan, Libya, and indeed elsewhere in places like Ukraine; all of these conflicts have their roots in the pursuit of power, land and control of resource.

The Arab Spring has now turned into a long winter of bloodshed and while the arms dealers get richer and the heads of government debate 'favourable' outcomes, innocent people continue to die.

This continued tragedy, death and destruction, witnessed by a world now far too accustomed to unrest, is often meted out on civilian populations by heavily armed military forces, reducing the life of the individual to expendable collateral damage, in what at times seem irresolvable conflicts. Human lives in different parts of the world are afforded different values and, like currencies, are there to be traded and spent with abandon.

The Green Party refuses to accept that people's lives in different parts of the world can ever have differing values and currencies, and equally rejects the disconnection politicians often promote between nation states and their peoples.

For most of us in the UK, the atrocities carried out in the pursuit of power, land or money are only ever pictures on a TV or one-liners on an internet posting, and many understandably switch channels or delete posts which trouble their conscience. It is clear to see that the behaviour of the rich – pop stars and actors and who they may or may not be sharing a bed with – has far more value than the plight of innocent families being blown to pieces by weaponry, often British-made, in the name of religion or regime change.

The public understandably run away from things that they don't wish to see: they know how horrible war can be, but they don't want to confront it head on, they don't want to look. It's not a question of denial; it's just natural not to want to constantly come face to face with such horrors. But even the pictures on our TV screens and in the newspapers are in themselves just a watered-down version of the horrid reality; we view death from not just a geographical distance but also from a digital one. This type of sanitised reporting is again a media-controlled response to people's discomfort with the whole truth.

Thankfully, though, despite this censorship we are seeing, the world is now facing up to the fact that 'something must be done'. But just what is the something that should be done? And how can the Green Party really make a difference?

Well, we could start by campaigning to stop the UK's arms sales within these regions and denying the grim reaper his scythe. We could, as a nation, once politicians work out how to spell disproportionate, call for more UN action, but we all know that every attempt to make states answerable to the world community is often thwarted by vetoes on UN votes. So then we are back to that whole human currency question again, in a politics-versus-people exchange rate system. So what else can we do? Or, more importantly, what is left for us to do that is worth trying and likely to succeed?

We certainly need to continue to promote diplomatic solutions to conflicts prior to the guns being loaded. We need to continue to support humanitarian and social support going into troubled regions.

Israel–Palestine

Take the Israel–Palestine conflict. The body count in Palestine continues to rise day by day, more protests bring more shootings and more killings, and yet Western governments still seem completely unable or unwilling to challenge the full extent of the Israeli government's brutality.

The completely vacuous comments tripped out to an overly biased press from world leaders including David Cameron in the UK simplistically repeat and reiterate 'Israel's right to defend itself' and give too prominent a focus to Hamas's futile rocket attacks. These sound bites are now little more than an embarrassment and an insult to a world community waking up to the realities of the increasingly one-sided nature of this horrific conflict.

Just how many innocent Palestinian civilians and children must die before those over-eager to support Israel realise that their inaction and carefully crafted words of comfort to Israel are in fact little less than an accessory to these brutal killings?

Yes, Israel is entitled to its security; yes, Hamas must stop firing its rockets; and yes, the loss of each and every Israeli life is equally to be condemned by us all. But surely, above all, the people of Palestine need world protection from a vicious Israeli government willing to kill innocents by way of collective punishment for the activities of a few. What other government occupies its neighbour's towns and cities and wantonly executes people protesting on their own land? Israel's breach of international law in support of its continued illegal occupation and resettlement of Palestinian land will only stop if those who have influence decide to use it.

While a continued and lasting peace remains, the world must also own and answer the wider questions of justice and accountability of all parties in relation to the atrocities carried out by both sides. Hamas's rocket attacks on Israel may be futile and dealt with at ease by Israel's Iron Dome defence system, but they are still indiscriminate acts of violence carried out by an elected government against a civilian population. Israel refuses to sign the International Convention on Human Rights, belittling the role of the International Criminal Court and prefers to play hardball with world concerns, so any complaint by them to the court prosecutor for investigation and trial of Hamas's actions are a non-starter. Palestine, however, is now a recognised UN state and can sign the convention, and it should ask the prosecutor to hold those responsible in Israel for giving the orders to butcher innocent children and families, to account.

Peace and reconciliation are non-negotiable partners; long-standing peace can never hold without tackling the thorny issues of justice and accountability head on. Such was the case in South Africa and Northern Ireland, and such, we hope, will be the case in Israel–Palestine.

The old adage 'No justice, no peace' may be an overused and underdelivered mantra, but for Palestine it will be a prerequisite for the acceptance of a permanent Israeli state as its neighbour and not its prisoner and executioner.

A full list of our international policies can be found online at www.policy.greenparty.org.uk/ip.html.

Tony Clarke is the Green Party's spokesperson on international affairs, and parliamentary candidate for Northampton North. He is a former Labour councillor, MP and chair of the Northern Ireland Select Committee. @tonyclarkeuk

Chapter 14

Animals

CAROLINE ALLEN

The Green Party believes we should live in a world where animals do not suffer cruelty and exploitation at the hands of humans. It is a key Green principle that animals – as sentient beings with an innate value of their own – are not ours to be used for any purpose where we might see a potential benefit for ourselves.

Voting Green sends a message that animals matter to you and that you believe that they all deserve respect. A Green vote gives a voice to the billions of animals worldwide that suffer silently, usually hidden from view. It is a vote not just for 'what is best for me' but a signal of a wider concern for living beings that are not commodities to be used however we see fit in this profit-driven world.

It is important to recognise that practices that harm animals often harm people too. There is a clear link between a system that tolerates, even encourages, the abuse of animals with one that mistreats people. The link between animal abuse and human violence is well known. When we look at the health effects of our intensive food system, the pollution caused by factory farming and the failure of animal testing to represent what happens in the human body it is clear that where animals are harmed, there is often harm to people too. This interconnectedness is important to Greens.

This position on the innate value of animals is reflected in our strong policies and the work of elected Greens and of Green campaigners across the country. We know that many people share our views on the importance of animal protection; sadly, other political parties do not. Even where they do make small steps in the right direction – such as the Hunting Act – these are often poorly implemented and in response to a single, high-profile campaign, rather than as a coordinated set of beliefs and policies.

Animal protection, when it is considered by other parties, is frequently seen as an add-on – but only if it doesn't impact other areas, or cost too much – rather than as a fundamental principle in its own right. The current government, with its insistence on pursuing the inhumane, unethical and scientifically illiterate badger cull and supporting the killing of protected species, is particularly poor on these issues. This is unsurprising given their treatment of the most vulnerable in society.

Factory farming: we all pay the price of cheap food

The case of factory farming is perhaps the perfect illustration of how appalling animal cruelty lies at the centre of a massive and growing industry that damages us all. Other political parties may tinker, but only Greens have a long-standing position of being completely opposed to factory farming. Our position is primarily due to the mistreatment of animals that is inherent in these systems, where animals are crowded together and abused in order to boost productivity. However, when we also look at the effect on our health and the environment, it redoubles our resolve.

Industrialisation of our food supply is sold to us as the way to feed a growing population. In reality it is nothing of the sort. The suffering of billions of animals is resulting in profit for the few, while the rest of us pay the true cost of cheap food.

The wider costs of this system of farming are great and are picked up by wider society, not by the industry itself. Increased levels of meat and dairy consumption that have resulted from the high production levels of industrial farming are a major factor in diet-related health problems. Much research now shows a link between overconsumption of animal products and cardiovascular disease, diabetes and certain cancers.[52] There is also evidence that factory-farmed meat and dairy is lower in important nutrients than free-range equivalents.

The environmental impact of these farms is massive and comprises local issues such as pollution from waste and excess water usage to effects much further afield. Industrial farming is highly reliant on fossil fuels and imported feed, driving deforestation and pushing up crop prices. Sixty per cent of EU and 33–40 per cent of global cereal production is used to feed animals: a highly inefficient way to produce food.[53] A UN Environment Programme report concluded that a kilo of cereals provides six times as many calories if eaten directly by people than if it is fed to livestock.

But even setting aside all of these major concerns, it is the systematic abuse of billions of animals in the pursuit of profit that has always meant that factory farming is unacceptable to Greens.

In the UK alone, more than 850 million animals are slaughtered for food every year, and the vast majority of these animals are farmed intensively. Animals are kept crowded together with inadequate space to express normal behaviours; they are under chronic stress and suffer disease as a result.

---

52 W. P. Castelli, 'The new pathophysiology of coronary artery disease', *American Journal of Cardiology*, 1998; 82 (10B): 60T–65T www.wcrf.org/int/research-we-fund/our-cancer-prevention-recommendations.
    G. Fagherazzi et al., 'Dietary acid load and risk of type 2 diabetes: the E3N-EPIC cohort study', *Diabetologia*, 14 October 2013.
    World Cancer Research Fund International. 'Recommendations for Cancer Prevention, Second Expert Report 2007', www.wcrf.org/int/research-we-fund/our-cancer-prevention-recommendations.
53 'World Livestock 2011: livestock in food security', UN Food and Agriculture Organization.

Suffering on top of suffering

The practice of performing 'mutilations', something that takes place on various types of factory farms, provides a very telling illustration of how the animals and their needs are viewed in this system.

An example of this is the beak trimming performed on hens. It is a natural behaviour for hens to peck; they do this in order to search for food and sample possible food items. Crowded together in a completely unnatural environment they are unable to perform this normal behaviour. Instead, some hens peck the feathers of other hens, which can lead to injury and even death; 'outbreaks' can occur with mortality rates in the region of 15 per cent.

Rather than see this abnormal behaviour as a clear sign that these birds are suffering and their needs not being met, the answer in the world of the factory farming industry is to cut off the beak of the hen. In doing so, highly sensitive tissues in the beak are damaged, leading to pain and sensitivity.[54] A ban is proposed for 2016 but this is threatened as the industry refuses to deal with the underlying issues and so says feather pecking will again become a problem.

The Green approach is clear, such mutilations must end and instead animals must be kept in ways where they can engage in their normal behaviours. The tinkering around the issues by proposing bans on cruel practices, then withdrawing them when the industry complains, is not only doing no good for the animals but risks misleading the public that progress is being made.

Other cruel practices associated with our current farming system include the large distances animals are transported before slaughter. South East England Green MEP Keith Taylor has been campaigning in Europe for animal transport time limits and against the resumption of live-animal exports from the ports of Dover and Ramsgate.

Undercover footage has also revealed significant animal suffering and abuse in UK slaughterhouses, including animals slaughtered for

54   P. Y. Hester and M. Shea-Moore, 'Beak trimming egg-laying strains of chickens', *World's Poultry Science Journal*, 59 (2003), pp. 458–74. doi:10.1079/WPS20030029.

organic meat. Greens support the campaign for mandatory CCTV in all slaughterhouses, with Green MP Caroline Lucas sponsoring an Early Day Motion in the House of Commons. As well as acting as a deterrent, CCTV will provide evidence for animal abuse prosecutions.

Save antibiotics for human health

We can't be sure exactly how many antibiotics are given to food animals because there is no requirement to report it, and we believe this must immediately change. The use of antibiotics to prop up a farming system where animals are kept in inhumane and completely unsuitable conditions, suffering great stress, is surely one of the great scandals of our time. Greens are supporters of the Alliance to Save Our Antibiotics and join them in calling for a ban on the routine use of antibiotics in farmed animals. There are now a significant number of studies that show how resistant bacteria are spreading from factory farms into the human population.[55] The Chief Medical Officer, Professor Dame Sally Davies, has warned that a post-antibiotic era is approaching. Are we really willing to risk our ability to perform chemotherapy, routine surgical procedures and treat infections so we can eat a cheap burger?

Frankenfood?

Selective breeding has already pushed animals beyond their natural limits in the pursuit of ever faster growth and production. Chickens grow much faster than they used to, reaching slaughter weight by forty-two days, and this change has led to a very high incidence of

---

55   F. J. Angulo, V. N. Nargund and T. C. Chiller, 'Evidence of an association between use of anti-microbial agents in food animals and anti-microbial resistance among bacteria isolated from humans and the human health consequences of such resistance', *Journal of Veterinary Medicine* Series B 51 (8–9) (2004), pp. 374–9.

leg weakness.[56] These conditions led the eminent welfare scientist
John Webster to say:

> We must conclude that approximately one-quarter of the heavy strains of
> broiler chickens and turkey are in chronic pain for approximately one-third
> of their lives. Given that poultry meat consumption in the UK exceeds
> 1 million tonnes per annum, this must constitute in both magnitude and
> severity the single most severe, systematic example of man's inhumanity
> to another sentient animal.

Cows now produce such high quantities of milk that they suffer
from very high incidences of mastitis (infection and inflammation
of the mammary gland), painful lameness and metabolic disease, all
related to the strain of producing much more milk than they would
naturally be expected to provide.

Now there are further technological 'advances' proposed that mod-
ify these living creatures, with little concern for the impact on them,
in order to maximise the characteristic that is valuable to us. Animals
are not commodities; they should not be bred or altered to become
grotesque living machines. We must return to the use of more traditional breeds and continue to oppose the use of growth hormones.
Greens oppose all genetic modification of animals and cloning.

It should be clear from the examples above – which are just a small
selection of the welfare problems associated with factory farming –
that this system is so completely at odds with a just and sustainable
world, the sort of world that Greens want to see. There is an alternative, which is based around smaller-scale free-range units, sustainable
farming methods, shorter food chains and support for local agriculture. Green policies support this alternative, along with encouraging
a move to a more plant-based diet with a reduction in consumption

---

56   S. C. Kestin, T. G. Knowles, A. E. Tinch, N. G. Gregory, 'Prevalence of leg weakness in
     broiler chickens and its relationship with genotype', *Veterinary Record*, no. 131 (1992),
     pp. 190–94.

of meat and dairy products, which would improve health and enable us to feed a growing global population much more easily.

Replacing animals in experiments

Greens oppose animal experimentation because we do not believe that animals should suffer – confined in barren environments, possibly undergoing painful procedures – for our own ends. Increasingly, the evidence also points to the fact that animal testing and experimentation may not be as beneficial to human health and scientific progress as we have been told.

Important progress has already been made in reducing the number of animals used in labs with the introduction of a Europe-wide ban on testing cosmetics on animals. The support of Greens in the European Parliament was pivotal to the success of this bill. This was a massive step which also had a far-reaching effect, as products tested outside the EU could also not be imported. The legislation also drove innovation in better ways of testing cosmetics.

Now the same progress needs to be made in the area of drug testing on animals, particularly because it is becoming increasingly clear that there is no scientific basis for it. A large-scale analysis of data provided by reputable biotech companies was used by researchers to make 3,200 comparisons of the effects of drugs in animals (dogs, rats, mice, rabbits) and humans.[57] They found that the absence of toxicity in animals provides essentially no insight into the likelihood of toxicity in humans. It is the presence of a negative result which decides whether the drug goes on through further testing, so this research raises very serious questions about the utility of this testing.

The case of the single-dose acute toxicity test also illustrates just how little real science there is behind animal testing. This test was

---

57　J. Bailey, M. Thew, M. Balls, 'An Analysis of the Use of Animal Models in Predicting Human Toxicology and Drug Safety', *ALTA: Alternatives to Laboratory Animals*, no. 42 (2014), pp. 181–99.

a key requirement of drug testing for decades until, in 2009, it was demonstrated that it had little scientific value in terms of identifying major organ toxicities and setting dose levels for subsequent studies. Shockingly, millions of rodents were being killed for a test with little value.

Only Greens are pushing for an end to this expensive and archaic system of testing, which has little basis in science. Animal testing not only causes suffering for the animals but wastes money and puts human lives at risk from adverse reactions. Ninety-two per cent of new drugs successful in animal studies go on to fail in clinical trials, while some that fail in animal testing would likely be useful in humans.

It is time for real innovation in this field that will benefit humans and animals alike. Exciting developments are occurring in advanced non-animal technologies areas including DNA chips, microfluidics chips, the use of human tissue, epidemiology, computer models, microdosing and advanced imaging. It is vital that we support and fund these areas, something Greens propose in the UK and across Europe.

In order to settle the debate over animal testing, Caroline Lucas cosponsored an Early Day Motion calling on the government to initiate a comparison of currently required animal tests with a set of human biology-based tests, as proposed in the Safety of Medicines (Evaluation) Bill 2009, to see which was the most effective means to predict the safety of medicines for patients. Unfortunately, the motion did not proceed. More Greens are definitely needed in Parliament.

On the issue of wider animal experimentation, it is also increasingly clear that the claim that animal experimentation is essential to medical development is not supported by scientific evidence. Of course, animal models have been of some use in specific cases – if you conduct millions of experiments, some are going to accurately predict human outcomes. However, where systematic reviews have been performed, they show that the utility of animal models for advancing human healthcare is very low and certainly not worth the cost in lost research funds, impacts on people affected by false predictions, and lab animal impacts.

Animal models for diseases are often misleading as animals do not get many of the diseases humans do, such as heart disease, many types of cancer, HIV, Parkinson's disease, or schizophrenia, so these have to be artificially induced. These techniques result in a 'model' that doesn't really amount to the same disease as humans. There are also physiological differences between humans and the lab animal. It is perhaps no surprise that there are numerous examples where medical progress has been delayed by poor animal 'models'.

When researchers looked at the usefulness of primate studies – which are difficult to get permission for and should therefore have a very good chance of leading to breakthroughs in people – the researchers 'showed that the majority of chimpanzee research is never subsequently cited in human medical studies. On the rare occasion that they were cited, it was clear that the chimpanzee experiments had contributed little, if anything, to the outcomes described in papers reporting an advance in human clinical practice.'[58] Caroline Lucas has supported the campaign to end the UK involvement in the cruel trade in wild-caught primates for research by sponsoring a parliamentary event and tabling an Early Day Motion (EDM 957).

In 2011, this statement was made in the *British Medical Journal*: 'The claim that animal experimentation is essential to medical development is not supported by proper, scientific evidence but by opinion and anecdote. Systematic reviews of its effectiveness don't support the claims made on its behalf.'[59] An increasing body of evidence seems to support this and, while as Greens our position on animal experimentation is an ethical one, we want to work in all ways possible not only to end these practices but to ensure that funds and research effort are directed to methods with the best outcome for people.

---

58   J. Bailey, 'Non-human primates in medical research and drug development: a critical review', *Biogenic Amines*, 19 (4–6) (2005), pp. 235–55.

59   P. Pound, S. Ebrahim, P. Sandercock, M. B. Bracken, I. Roberts, 'Where is the evidence that animal research benefits humans?' *British Medical Journal*, no. 328 (28 February 2004), pp. 514–17.

Protecting nature

Recent reports have suggested that global animal populations have halved in the last forty years. This is a truly shocking figure. Habitat loss and illegal wildlife trade, combined with unsustainable legal trade, are devastating species across the globe and climate change will only accelerate declines. We need urgent action to protect habitats and the animals in them, and we need real action on climate change. Only Greens have shown genuine commitment to these issues, both nationally and within the EU.

The other parties see nature, climate action, biodiversity and wildlife protection as an optional 'nice to have'; something to look at once the economy is 'back on track'. They do not understand that if we do not tackle these interlinked problems then the economic outcome will be catastrophic. Never mind that the current economic system, with the drive to growth at all costs, is the main cause of these problems.

A recent report revealed that 60 per cent of the species studied have declined over recent decades in the UK. More than one in ten of all the species assessed are under threat of disappearing from our shores altogether.[60] This has led to major UK wildlife charities to call for the introduction of a Nature and Well-being Act, something the Green Party supports.

Included in the Act would be a long-term commitment to specific targets for nature's recovery and an effective mechanism for creating a national ecological network. Specific targets would be set to ensure that people and especially children are able to connect to nature. Nature would need to be considered in decision-making and when writing new laws.

One thing the Green Party is very clear on is that nature and wildlife has a value beyond just the financial and that its loss cannot be justified on the basis of a calculation of economic benefit. Insects may not get much attention but they are vital to our ecosystems.

60   State of Nature Report, 2013, www.rspb.org.uk/Images/stateofnature_tcm9-345839. pdf, accessed 12 December 2014.

Greens in the European Parliament have been heavily involved in action to ban pesticides suspected to harm pollinators.

Wildlife crime is a serious and growing issue, both in the UK and overseas, with links to large criminal syndicates, threatening the very survival of species such as rhino and elephant. Greens in the UK and Europe have worked extensively on the issue of the illegal wildlife trade and also unsustainable legal trade. We are calling for much greater support for developing countries in developing effective wildlife-law enforcement and more multinational action (e.g. Interpol Wildlife Crime Unit). Green Party London Assembly Member Jenny Jones played a pivotal role in saving the Metropolitan Police Wildlife Crime Unit. We support a ban on the import of all wild-caught animals.

As an MEP, Caroline Lucas was one of the sponsors of the legislation that led to the ban on the import of seal products into the EU. It came into force in 2010 and will save hundreds of thousands of seals from slaughter. The Green Party will continue to work towards a full ban on the import of all fur products.

Strengthen the Hunting Act

The Hunting Act is very popular legislation, but it needs to be properly enforced and loopholes removed. Any attempt to repeal it will be resisted strongly by the Green Party. We are fundamentally opposed to all blood sports and would extend legislation to prohibit shooting, snaring, coursing and other abuses of wild animal populations.

Stop the pointless badger cull

Greens have been heavily involved in campaigning against the badger cull from the very start, in Parliament, on badger patrols and as part of the wider campaigning movement. It is inhumane, unethical and unlikely to have an impact on the prevalence of bTB (bovine tuberculosis) in cattle. The government's obsession with this policy – which goes against the advice of independent scientists – has wasted years and millions of pounds and has left farmers still dealing with bTB. Meanwhile evidence from Wales[61] – where they have not culled badgers but focused on strict cattle-control measures – shows a significant reduction in bTB cases. We will continue to oppose this policy and work at a European level to allow for quicker approval of any vaccine to protect cattle against bovine TB.

A nation of animal lovers?

The over-breeding and irresponsible ownership of dogs in the UK has reached unprecedented levels. The year 2011 saw the highest ever recorded number of stray and abandoned dogs in the UK at 127,000, of which it is reported that 7,000 dogs were destroyed. That figure has fallen slightly to 112,000 in 2013 but this is clearly still a massive issue, especially given that these figures are likely to be underestimates.

At the same time, puppies are bred in appalling conditions on puppy farms, both here and overseas, from where they are often illegally imported.

The Green Party is calling for much tighter regulation for the pet industry. We aim to end puppy farming by banning the sale of young puppies and kittens unless the mother is present, and by licensing all animal breeders and dog owners, with a two-tier system of dog-licensing (breeding and non-breeding) linked to compulsory microchipping. We would also take action on breeding to prevent exaggerated characteristics likely to cause suffering.

The exotic pet trade is a great source of suffering. A 2012 study of the exotic pet trade found that at least 75 per cent of pet snakes, lizards, tortoises and turtles died within one year.[62] The lifespan of the

---

61   www.wales.gov.uk/statistics-and-research/incidence-tuberculosis-cattle-great-britain/?lang=en, accessed 12 December 2014.

62   E. Toland, C. Warwick and P. C. Arena, 'The exotic pet trade: pet hate', *The Biologist*, vol. 59, issue 3 (2012), pp. 14–18.

species involved should range from eight to 120 years. It is thought that most of these died from captivity stress-related causes. Many, many more animals die before they even reach the pet store. It is clear that this trade is unsustainable and, as such, Greens are working to end the keeping of exotic pets, including primates.

Animal suffering isn't entertainment

Nearly three British citizens out of every four support a ban on wild animals in circuses. Animals do not belong on the road, living in inadequate enclosures, suffering from inappropriate, sometimes cruel, training techniques and performing routines that demean them and their audience. We would ban the use of all animals in circuses.

The Green Party will also end the exploitation of animals in horse racing and greyhound racing. Greens have been involved in campaigns to shut down greyhound tracks and also to highlight the very high levels of injury and death associated with horse racing.

Summary

Sadly, there are too many circumstances where animals suffer due to human actions to cover them all here. Summarising some of the key problems and Green solutions hopefully illustrates our philosophy and the need for a more humane approach in general.

We believe our approach is beneficial not only to animals, but also to people and the environment – so everybody wins.

Caroline Allen is a practising vet and the Green Party's spokesperson on animals. She has campaigned on a wide range of animal issues and has a special interest in food and farming policy. @Green_Caroline

Appendix

The Green Party's Core Values

The Green Party isn't just another political party. Green politics is a new and radical kind of politics guided by these ten core principles:

The Green Party is a party of social and environmental justice, which supports a radical transformation of society for the benefit of all, and for the planet as a whole. We understand that the threats to economic, social and environmental well-being are part of the same problem, and recognise that solving one of these crises cannot be achieved without solving the others.

Humankind depends on the diversity of the natural world for its existence. We do not believe that other species are expendable.

The Earth's physical resources are finite. We threaten our future if we try to live beyond those means, so we must build a sustainable society that guarantees our long-term future.

Every person, in this and future generations, should be entitled to basic material security as of right.

Our actions should take account of the well-being of other nations, other species, and future generations. We should not pursue our well-being to the detriment of theirs.

A healthy society is based on voluntary co-operation between empowered individuals in a democratic society, free from discrimination, whether based on race, colour, gender, sexual orientation, religion, social origin or any other prejudice.

We emphasise democratic participation and accountability by

ensuring that decisions are taken at the closest practical level to those affected by them.

We look for non-violent solutions to conflict situations, which take into account the interests of minorities and future generations in order to achieve lasting settlements.

The success of a society cannot be measured by narrow economic indicators but should take account of factors affecting the quality of life for all people: personal freedom, social equity, health, happiness and human fulfilment.

Electoral politics is not the only way to achieve change in society, and we will use a variety of methods, including lifestyle changes, to help effect progress, providing those methods do not conflict with our other core principles.

Acknowledgements

I thank the contributors for the aplomb with which they approached the commission. Such is the importance to Greens of having our policies showcased. Life as editor was made far happier as a result. I am also grateful to David Flint and Jack Terry for editorial assistance.

I thank Biteback for having the gumption to include us in the series. Our exclusion from TV election debates has become a political question in its own right and it is affirming to be treated on a par here. Thanks to all the team, in particular Iain Dale and Olivia Beattie.

I thank party members and activists over the years for making the party such a vital force for electoral good. Without their collective wisdom and resolve, our politics would not be as vibrant and relevant as it now is. Regular conversations and encounters with comrades sustain me. I can't list all, but particular thanks to Martin Francis, Siân Berry, Mike Gubbins, Amelia Womack, Noel Lynch, Jenny Jones and Scott Bartle.

Finally, I thank Sevara for her support in more ways than I can say. I was once described as married to the Green Party. I've since married in real life, but somehow feel able to pursue politics with equal if not greater resolve.

About the Editor

Dr Shahrar Ali was elected deputy leader of the Green Party in September 2014, in the process becoming the first BME deputy of a UK parliamentary party. He entered green politics after working as a researcher in the European Parliament on the risk of GM foods. He has a PhD in philosophy, in which he tackled the morality of lying and deception, with special attention to public life. He is author of *Why Vote Green* (2010), an impassioned call for environmental action and social transformation, and is standing for Brent Central at the next general election. www.shahrarali.net @ShahrarAli